100% UNOFFICIAL

ROBLOX

CREATE AND CONQUER!

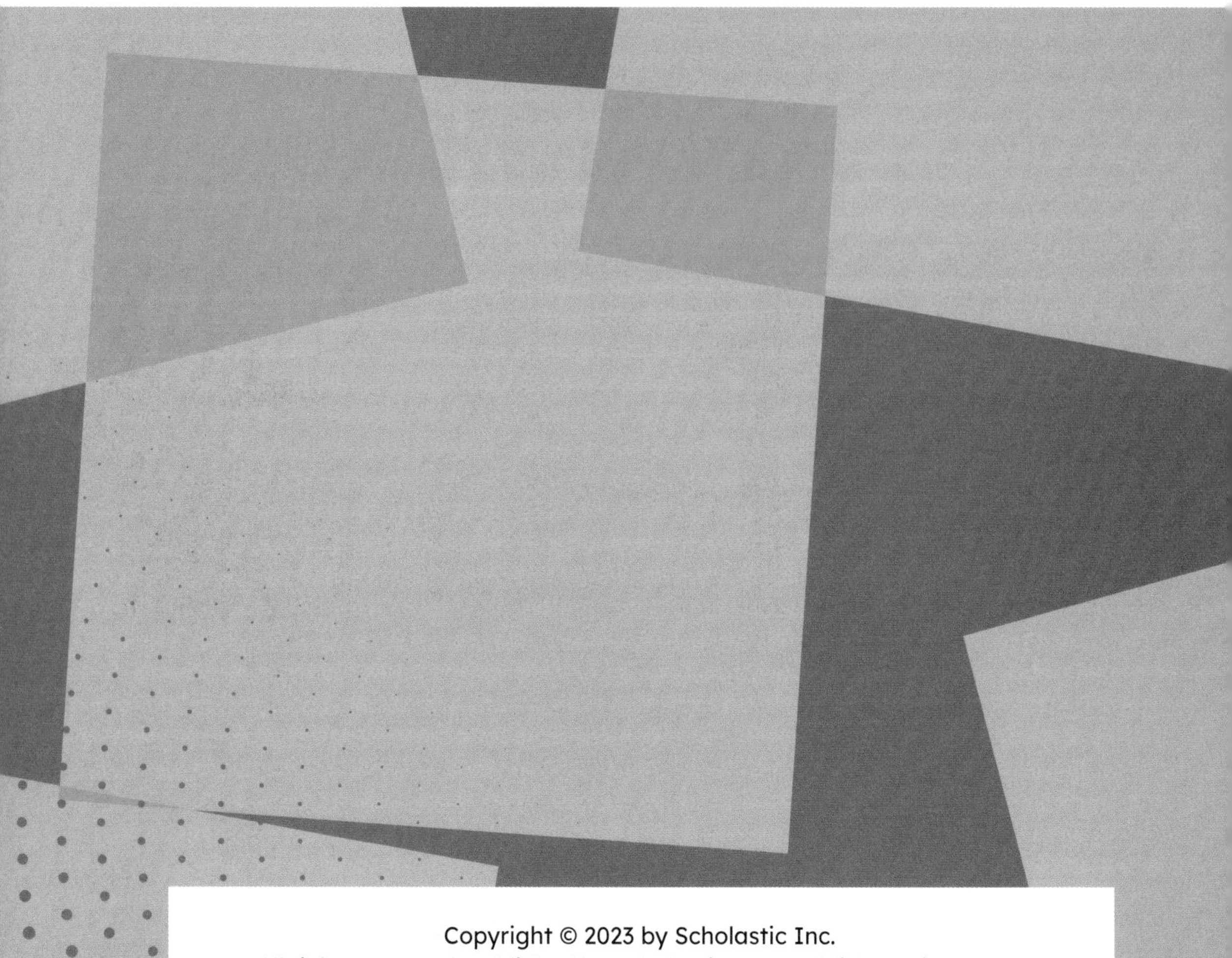

ISBN 978-1-338-89308-3

10 9 8 7 6 5 4 3 2 1 23 24 25 26 27

Printed in the U.S.A. 40
First printing 2023

100% UNOFFICIAL
ROBLOX

CREATE AND CONQUER!

SCHOLASTIC INC.

CONTENTS

DO YOU SPEAK BLOX?

Learn this lingo so you don't stand out as a total noob!

bloxxed

Getting killed in a Roblox game (meaning your avatar falls into pieces).

comped

Short for "compromised," this means an account that's been hacked!

GG

An abbreviation of "good game"! Used in chat after playing with, or against, another person.

harvest

To collect items in a game, which you can sell, craft, or use.

NPC

Non-player character. A character controlled by the game itself.

noob

Someone who's new to a game—or to Roblox itself!—and hasn't gotten the hang of it yet.

obby

An obstacle-based game—the simplest and most common type of game in Roblox.

OP

An abbreviation of "overpowered," referring to items or weapons in a game that are a bit *too* useful and give too much of an advantage to whoever has them.

spawn

How a player, character, or item arrives in the game. If something "respawns," that means it reappears in the game after being destroyed or used—like a player who dies and returns to the map.

termed

A user who's been banned from Roblox.

XP

A kind of abbreviation of "experience points"—rewards in a game for completing tasks and performing actions.

NOOB? START HERE!

WHAT IS ROBLOX?

Roblox is an online platform for playing and making computer games, with over 200 million people worldwide using it every month. If you're new to Roblox, getting into it is easy!

HOW DO YOU PLAY?

You need access to a Windows PC, an Apple Mac, an Android or iOS device, or an Xbox (One, Series X, or Series S). It will really help if your PC or Mac is an up-to-date gaming-quality one. Roblox will run on lower-spec models, but it may be very slow—and Roblox Studio will run much better on a good gaming machine.

ROBLOX.COM

Go to Roblox.com and fill out the sign-up form. Have your parent or guardian with you to help choose a username and password. Don't use your real name as a username, for online safety reasons.

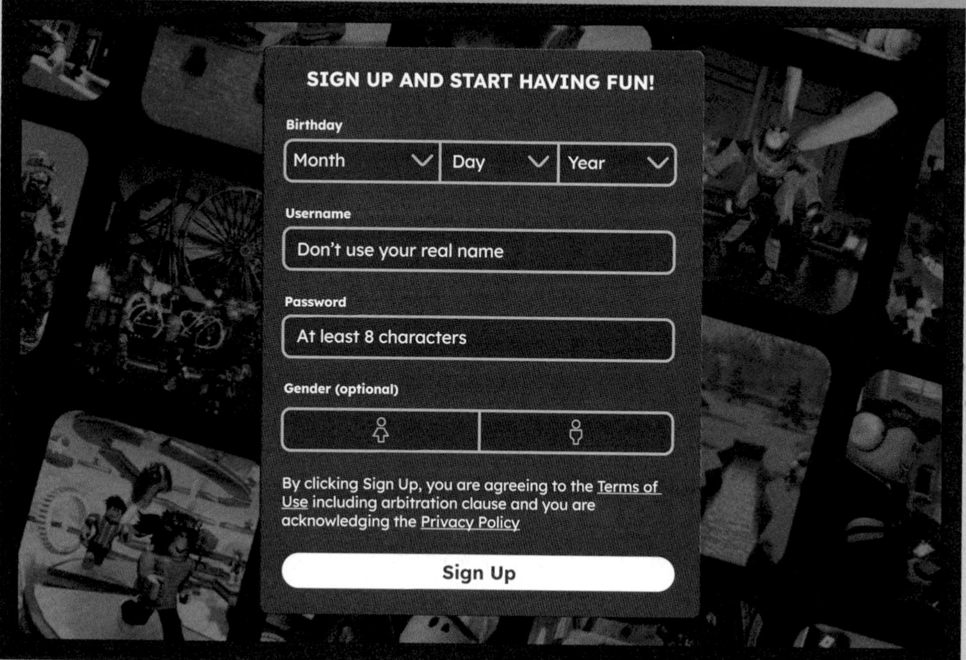

PASSWORD PROTECTION

It's very important to have a secure password and only enter it when logging in! Roblox will never ask for your password at any other time—if you get asked for your password in the middle of a game, someone's trying to scam you.

READY TO LAUNCH

Now you can go to your device's store and download the Roblox launcher for free. You can also buy Robux, the currency of Roblox—but you don't have to. You can just enjoy the games!

GETTING ALL DRESSED UP

You can choose clothes for your avatar from a selection of free items or by purchasing more items with Robux—*or* you can make your own clothing!

By far the easiest type of clothing to make is a T-shirt—it's also free to upload.

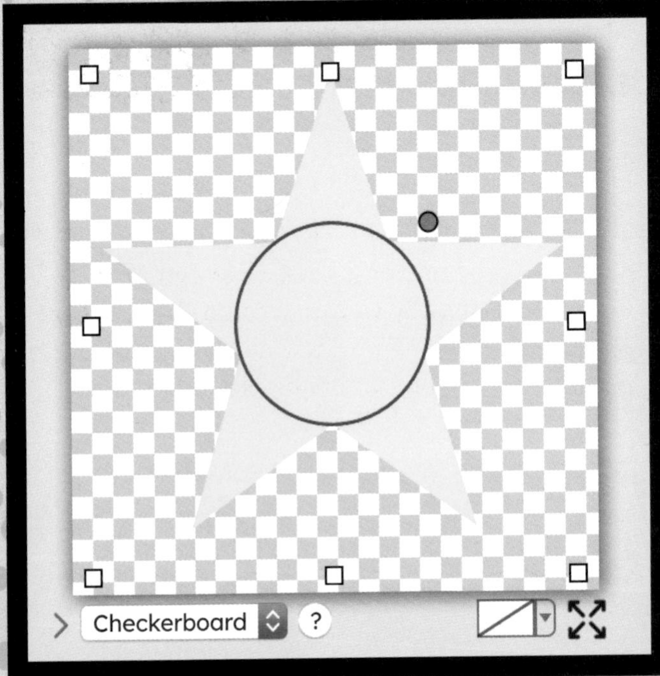

First you need to make an image—it should be a square image, 512 x 512 pixels. If it's a different size or shape, it'll get stretched or squashed to fit. It's easy to do this in any desktop art software, like MS Paint—you can set the height and width in pixels.

Now go to the Create tab on the Roblox site. (You may need to click on "Manage My Experiences.") Scroll down to T-shirts and you'll be able to create one by uploading your image. It might take a few minutes for the preview to appear.

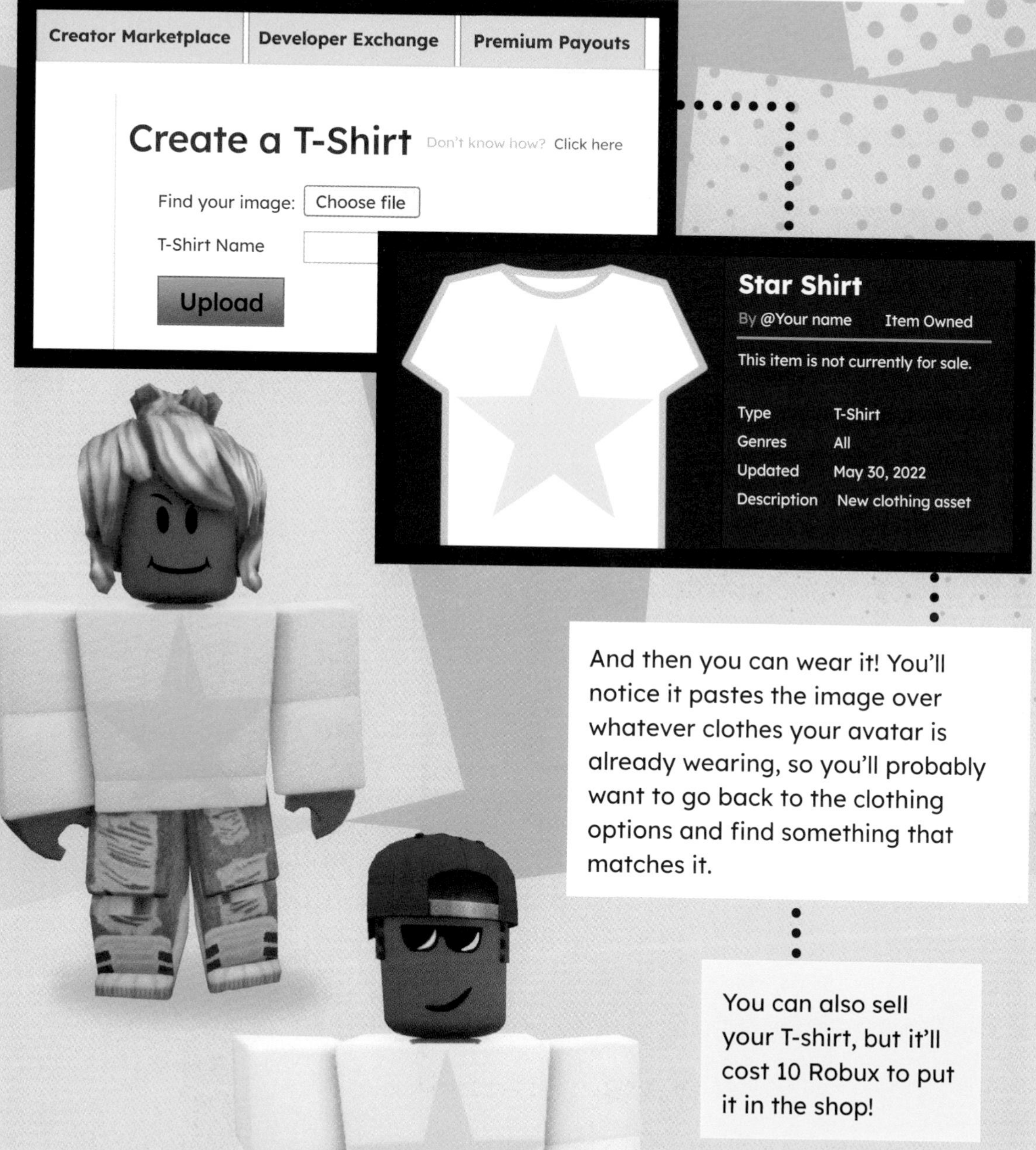

And then you can wear it! You'll notice it pastes the image over whatever clothes your avatar is already wearing, so you'll probably want to go back to the clothing options and find something that matches it.

You can also sell your T-shirt, but it'll cost 10 Robux to put it in the shop!

If you want to make a shirt or a pair of pants, it's trickier to do—and it'll cost you 10 Robux to upload.

The important thing to remember is that your clothes need to be *exactly* the right size and shape—if they're not, the uploader will reject them. So you'll need to download the official Shirt and Pants Templates.

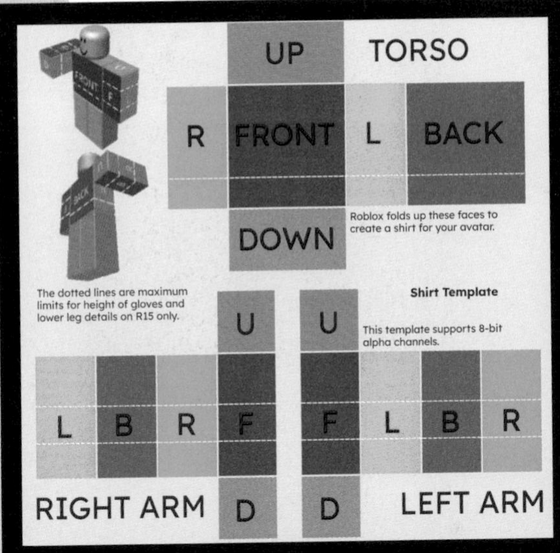

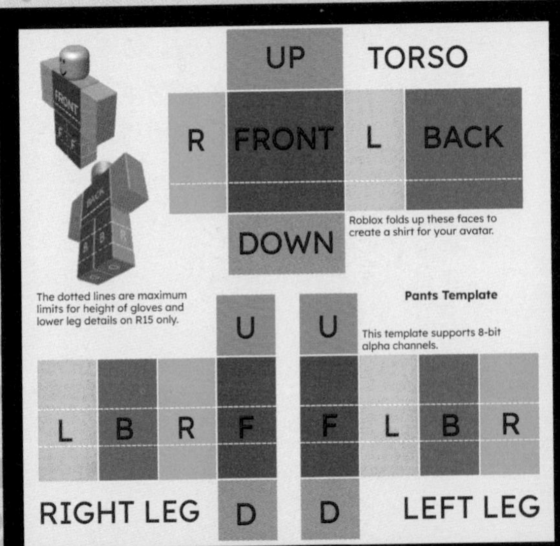

Now, you don't want to spend Robux to upload your new clothes and then find they don't look right—so test them out without paying in Roblox Studio. Download Studio if you don't already have it (see page 86 for more details).

Open the template in MS Paint, or whatever art program you use, and change the template to add your design into it. Just make sure you keep inside the lines! The uploader will know to ignore all the other stuff on the template.

Now go to the Plugins tab and select Build Rig, which should bring up a dummy avatar. Then go to the Explorer window and click Dummy, then click the plus sign. Find the clothing option (Shirt or Pants) and click on that.

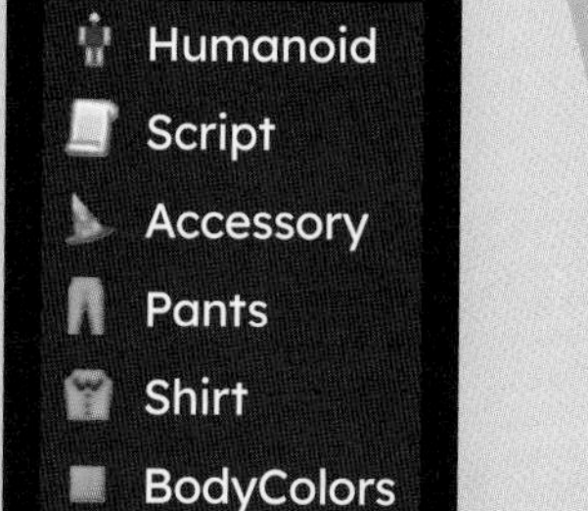

Inside the clothing item, click "ShirtTemplate" or "PantsTemplate" and upload your design! Now you can take a good look, and if it's not right, you can go back to your template and tweak it.

BLOX LIFE

GROW-BLOX

Roblox was already huge and growing before the COVID-19 pandemic—but, as people across the world were required to lock down and stay at home, many flocked to the platform. Roblox had around 120 million members at the end of 2019, and then an astonishing 80 million new people joined in 2020.

HANGOUT ZONE

The social side of Roblox became a lifeline for lots of people. Many of the most popular games are more like hangout spaces than conventional games, and that has helped make it a major part of people's lives.

LET'S DANCE

Increasingly, developers are embracing spaces like this—and making them bigger and more immersive. *Beatland*, which launched in 2022, allows players to enter a city with its own cinema, club, and record shop. You can get a job there—or just go and watch an animated film or a DJ set.

IN THE GROOVE

In fact, music has become a pretty big feature of the platform, with musicians like Lizzo, Lil Nas X, and Twenty One Pilots holding virtual concerts. In 2022, the BRIT Awards invited users to a VIP party on Roblox.

FUTURE BLOX

GETTING OLDER

The number of under-16s using Roblox is already super high. Some estimates say half of all under-16s in the USA use it! So the platform is particularly interested in expanding into older age groups. Currently, only about a third of users are over 16.

PROFESSIONAL STUDIOS

There are now 9.5 million developers on Roblox. Many of them are just making simple obbys for fun—there are over 40 million games, which means a lot of people have only made one or two games! But there are also professional studios that now specialize in working with the platform and can do surprising things with it.

AT THE FOREFRONT

There's no doubt Roblox is being taken more seriously now, as developers and companies realize what a great way it is to reach people—especially young people.

BLOX BRANDS

Roblox has often been home to unofficial fan-made games and parodies of popular movies, games, and TV shows. But increasingly, big brands and characters are realizing that if people are making these unofficial games, it means there's demand for official ones—and so they're doing it themselves.

WONDER KITTY

My Hello Kitty Cafe uses the familiar tycoon format to let players build and run their own *Hello Kitty* Cafe. An official *Wonder Woman* game lets you explore her home island of Themyscira. Even established game franchises like *Sonic the Hedgehog* have launched Roblox titles!

METAVERSE

There's been a lot of excitement lately about the potential of the metaverse (virtual social spaces), which could become extensions of existing social media. But Roblox has already been doing this for years!

VIRTUAL REALITY

The next step might be for VR headsets to become a bigger part of the experience. Headsets like the Oculus Rift can already be used with Roblox—they're not cheap, and they may not work with everyone's setup, but they have the potential to make Roblox even more interactive.

MAKE YOUR OWN

The ability to build your own space in Roblox seems likely to become a bigger part of the experience. You won't just be able to visit other places; you'll also be able to invite people to yours!

SO MANY GAMES

But for all the changes that have happened, the appeal of Roblox is the same as it's always been. First, most games on the platform are free to play, so you can try a huge number of them for no cost.

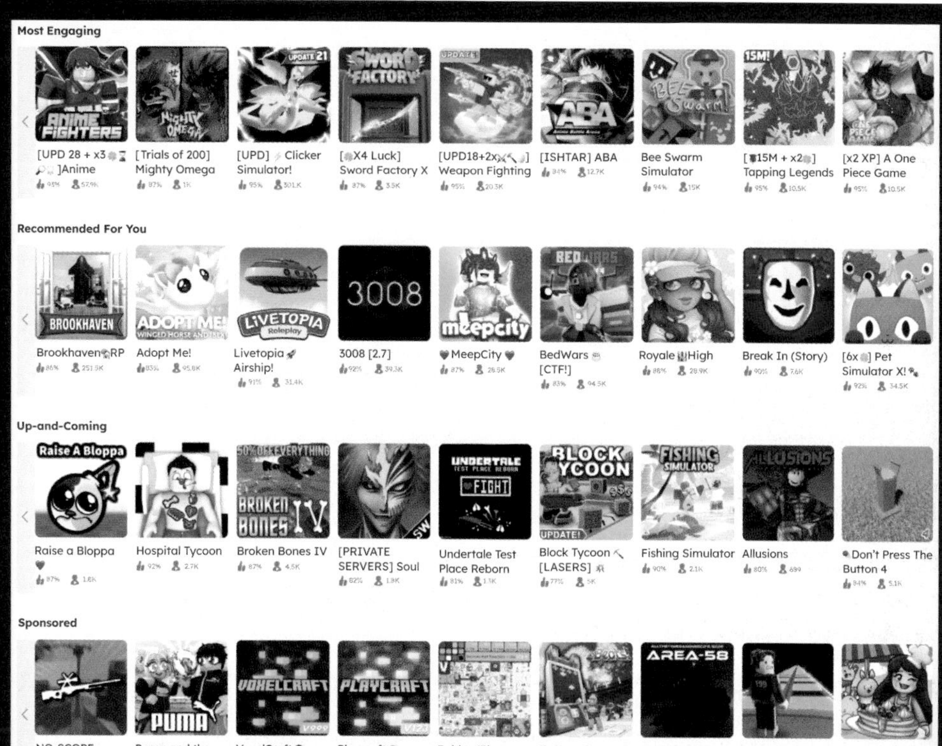

FOR EVERYONE!

And second, anyone can make a Roblox game and upload it for everyone to play. Those two things together make it the most open and accessible gaming system out there!

HOTTEST GAMES

New games are being uploaded to Roblox every day, and some of the most popular ones have only emerged in the last couple of years. Here's a look at some of the biggest hit games since the Great Roblox Surge of 2020 . . .

HOTTEST GAMES

The fast-moving world of Roblox brings new games all the time—and it's always cool to get into games before your friends do. In fact, it's more than cool—it can be really useful to have your character already at a high level while everyone else is scrambling to catch up!

FOLLOW A DEVELOPER

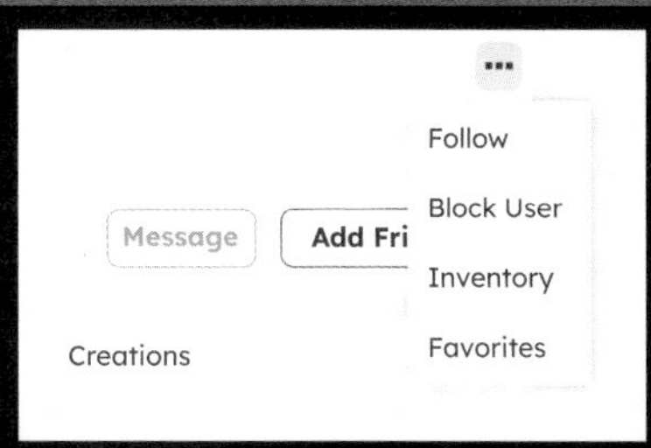

One way of spotting the latest games as they come up is to follow your favorite developers. Some developers focus on maintaining one game, but some—especially the bigger studios—will keep launching new ones. If you like a developer's work, look out for what they're doing next.

UP-AND-COMING

The Discover page in the Roblox catalog has a section marked "Up-and-Coming," which lists games that are rising in popularity. Skip past the clones of other hit games in this section and look for games offering something new and different.

UNOFFICIAL

Be aware that any unofficial game based on a popular film or TV show will probably get struck down for copyright reasons once it gets popular enough to be noticed, and will either be changed or taken down completely.

WORD OF MOUTH

A lot of Roblox games become big through word of mouth—so look out for what other people are recommending, and don't just rely on the algorithm to bring games to your attention!

By RELL World

10 SHINDO LIFE

One of the most popular sources of inspiration for Roblox games is manga and anime, and *Shindo Life* was originally based on *Naruto*—the first version of it was called *Shinobi Life*. You play as a ninja, exploring the game's open world, leveling up your skills, and battling bosses.

The character design is excellent, really showing off what's possible in Roblox. It's easy to see why it has become one of the most popular games—it's got a lot of depth to it and keeps players coming back for more.

MAKE SURE YOU EXPLORE . . .

BLOX TIP

Codes offering free coins and spins are always being issued in *Shindo Life*—keep a look out for new ones every month!

By Chillz Studios

BUILD A BOAT FOR TREASURE

One of the best treasure-hunting games on Roblox, *Build a Boat for Treasure* is a sandbox game with elements of *Minecraft*. You need to look for materials to build your boat and then you can use it to search for treasure. (Don't you love Roblox game titles that tell you everything you need to know?)

Perhaps the game's best feature is its co-op mode, which enables you to start a game with friends to build and sail the ship together. And the game keeps developing because you can unlock stuff during your search, which enhances the ship.

DOES ANYONE HAVE THE TIME?

BLOX TIP

When you put a chair on your boat, place a roof over it. This will save you if the boat flips.

8

By Vows by the Sea

DEEPWOKEN

We're mostly recommending free-to-play games, but *Deepwoken* really deserves a mention here. It costs 400 Robux—but, before you pay, be warned—it's not an easy game! Your character can permanently die, sending you to the Depths.

It's an open-world fantasy exploration game, but here's the twist—instead of filling in the map, there is no map. You just have to make your way through its detailed world of seas and islands without one! It's engrossing stuff, full of mysteries to discover—just watch your step . . .

AVOID THE DEPTHS.

BLOX TIP

It's possible to escape the Depths, but you'll need to ring all the bells in the City of the Drowned first. When you hear the biggest bell ring, go to the cathedral and take the elevator up to face a trial.

By Fireheart Studio

7 DEMONFALL

Inspired by the manga *Demon Slayer*, this game starts with you facing a demon. If you kill it, you become a slayer—if you fail, you'll be killed and sent to a hell dimension, turned into a demon, and cursed to consume human flesh. Not a great start to the day.

Demonfall is one of the most atmospheric games you'll find on Roblox, with impressive graphics and music, and it's got a huge map and lots of NPCs to talk to. The amount of travel can be a drag, but overall this is a fascinating game.

SLAY THE DEMONS TO STAY OUT OF HELL.

BLOX TIP

Kaigaku respawns randomly in Hayakawa and Okuyia, and drops 5,000 XP when beaten. So you can farm him for XP by beating him repeatedly—but he's best tackled by a group.

By Gamer Robot Inc

6 BLOX FRUITS

Another manga-inspired game—this time the source is *One Piece*, the long-running story of a pirate whose body was made stretchy and rubbery thanks to an encounter with a magic fruit. *Blox Fruits* is a quest-based game in which you choose to be on the side of the pirates or the marines, and you must earn money for weapons, ships—and fruit!

When you hit level 20, you can unlock PvP action, and that's when it gets really fun—you can team up with friends, roam around, and do quests together, but you can also attack other players!

TRAIN HARD AND LEVEL UP.

BLOX TIP

Save up to buy the Chop fruit as early as you can—it makes you immune to sword damage.

By BlockZone

5 ANIME FIGHTING SIMULATOR

This game is all about training and fighting, and it features characters and worlds inspired by popular anime like *Dragon Ball*, *My Hero Academia*, and *Attack on Titan*. While you start off with pretty basic sword-and-punching skills, you can train up and acquire new ones.

The quests and storylines mean there's lots to do beyond just leveling up your fighter and unlocking new skins. There are different modes, too, making this an easy game to get hooked on.

UNLEASH YOUR ANIME POWERS!

BLOX TIP

Stay in the safe zone until you've trained up to a decent level—other players will take down a noob pretty quickly!

By Top Down Games

4 ALL STAR TOWER DEFENSE

Tower defense games are another big Roblox genre, and *All Star Tower Defense* has emerged as the most popular. It has a variety of modes and maps, plus characters you can collect through the game's gacha system (a bit like the one in *Genshin Impact*).

COLLECT FAMILIAR ANIME FRIENDS.

In each map, you're tasked with protecting a place from waves of enemy attacks by deploying your own forces against them. The fun part in *All Star* is the locations and characters are taken from famous anime, which adds an extra dimension to its story mode.

BLOX TIP

You'll need to upgrade your forces around the third or fourth wave, otherwise the "Powerful" enemies that start to appear will get past them.

By Gamefam x Sonic

SONIC SPEED SIMULATOR

So, this is a pretty big deal—the first major game franchise to make a game specifically for Roblox. And *Sonic Speed Simulator* is great! It's clear how much work has gone into adapting Roblox's graphics to make this look like a *Sonic* game.

You start off playing as your usual Roblox self, and you'll be incredibly slow. But as you level up, you can increase your speed and actually compete in races. You can also collect characters to play as—and then it *really* starts to feel like *Sonic*!

GAIN *SONIC* SPEEDS!

BLOX TIP

A Sonic card will appear on a grind rail that starts near one of the big loops. You can bounce up to this rail by hitting the red launcher that's on the other side of this loop, once you've leveled up enough to jump up there. Then you can play as Sonic!

By @Wolfpaq

2 BROOKHAVEN RP

Social or real-life RPG games have been big on Roblox for a while now, and *Brookhaven RP* has emerged as one of the most popular. In fact, it's one of the most popular games on the platform, period.

CHILL OUT VIBES APLENTY!

Good design work is a big reason for this, such as the cool and modern houses you get at the start—they're just a nice place to hang out. It's slightly annoying that you need to pay to unlock the music, though! You can also create a private server by paying 100 Robux.

BLOX TIP

You can find a code to access a movie that reveals secrets about Brookhaven by driving down the road past the diner and the airport, and on to an abandoned house.

By @ColonelGraff

1 SCUBA DIVING AT QUILL LAKE

Looking for something to chill you out after a little too much time playing survival horror games? Look no further than *Scuba Diving at Quill Lake*. This is a nice game where you go scuba diving at a scenic lake. It's been around a long time but has soared in popularity in recent years.

It's more than just a relaxing experience—you search for lost pirate treasure, which will pay for equipment and training that in turn will enable you to unlock more areas, such as deeper water and dark, submerged caves.

DEEP DIVE FOR LOST TREASURE.

BLOX TIP

It's wise to make the geolocator your first purchase (it provides coordinates for each piece of treasure), and then the flashlight.

HOTTEST GAMES QUIZ

What type of character do you play as in *Shindo Life*?

What will save you if your boat flips in *Build a Boat for Treasure*?

3

How much does it cost to play *Deepwoken*?

4

How much XP does Kaigaku drop in *Demonfall*?

At what level in *Blox Fruits* can you unlock PvP?

Name an anime that's referenced in *Anime Fighting Simulator*.

7

What system is used in *All Star Tower Defense* to get new characters?

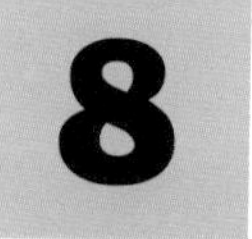

Where's the Sonic card in *Sonic Speed Simulator*?

9

How do you create a *Brookhaven RP* private server?

What's the most popular place to go scuba diving in Roblox?

WEIRD GAMES

Ever dug deep into the Roblox game catalog and found something that makes you think, *Er . . . what?!* Well, so have we. Join us for a journey into the stranger side of Roblox . . .

WEIRD GAMES

Usually, making a computer game is an expensive business involving lots of work from lots of highly skilled people. Companies making them want to be sure they look slick and professional, and appeal to the widest possible audience.

LET'S GET WEIRD

By making it easier to create a game, Roblox has opened the door to people who have weird, silly, or ridiculous ideas, giving them the tools to make those ideas a reality. Games that a professional company wouldn't release (and might not even understand) are now out there, thanks to Roblox!

TALK OF THE TOWN

A lot of weird games on the platform aren't totally finished, or even playable. But the best ones spread through word of mouth and become essential Roblox experiences—even if you only play them once.

ANYTHING CAN HAPPEN

The cool thing about playing weird Roblox games is that, even if they don't completely work, they do unexpected things and can change your ideas about what a game can be.

TRIED AND TESTED

A lot of games on Roblox are pretty similar to each other—we've all seen those clones of popular games—and it's refreshing to play something different. If you're a budding Roblox developer, they might even provide inspiration for your own games!

By @Radalkcor

10 DANCING PARROTS

Not exactly a game—more a pleasantly chill experience—but everyone should give it a try. You'll particularly enjoy it if you like watching the parrots dance in *Minecraft,* because that's basically what this is—parrots who look just like the *Minecraft* ones, on a stage, dancing to upbeat techno music.

SHAKE YOUR TAIL FEATHERS!

BLOX TIP

You can't go wrong! There are no winners here, no points to score. The winner is the player who gains the most joy from watching the parrots.

By @ArianaGrawnde

9 SURVIVE ARIANA GRANDE IN AREA 51

This game is set in Area 51, the US Air Force facility that's been the center of UFO conspiracy theories for decades. But here it's populated with murderous clones of Ariana Grande, which the player must avoid for as long as possible.

The game is free to play, but to successfully take on the clones, you'll need to splash out some Robux on a rocket launcher.

GREAT VOICE, TERRIBLE MANNERS...

BLOX TIP

Earn the Nicki Minaj badge by heading straight through the facility until you reach two doors opposite each other. Go through the left one and on to the radioactive area. Climb the pile of dirt next to the radioactive waste and use the ladder to enter the dirt tunnels until you find Nicki.

By @Rdite

8 HUMAN GIRAFFE

"A philosophical game on the nature of Robloxians" is how *Human Giraffe* describes itself. You're dropped into a landscape full of odd stuff like hamster wheels and space rockets. Oh, and your avatar now has a long, floppy neck.

And so you run around, living life with a long, floppy neck. See how the different things in the landscape affect your neck. Use your tongue to help you get around (yes, really). Enter the PvP arena. You can even unlock other options, such as Worm Mode, with Robux. It is a bit disturbing, though. You've been warned.

ARE YOU A HUMAN? OR A GIRAFFE?

BLOX TIP

Meerkat Mode gives you a straight neck—more like a giraffe, in fact—but using it can make the game go buggy, so you're better off sticking with the regular neck.

By thunder1222 Productions

7 MEGA NOOB SIMULATOR

In this fighting game, you start as a tiny weakling. But by seeking out and beating up hapless Bacons (guys with streaky hair), you can bulk up and become the Biggest Noob, growing your muscles to ridiculous size as you pound those Bacons into the ground.

It's extremely silly, but making progress is fun. You unlock new areas of the map as you reach new levels of strength, and head for the big showdown with King Bacon. There are also lots of things you can buy to make your Noob unique.

POUND THAT BACON!

BLOX TIP

When you have to take on Bionic Bacon, the best place to stand is between his legs.

By @Nimblz

6 EG!

Eg! is a wonderfully odd game of light adventure and exploration, in which you play as an egg. With legs. And a face. The main aim is to collect coins, which you can use to buy items for your egg, including hats, faces, colors, and pets—or you can just find the items while exploring.

There are also three keys to locate, which can be accessed via challenges in hidden locations, and a set of portals in the village where you spawn, which can be unlocked to enable you to travel to other worlds.

Hi!

YOU'LL HAVE AN EGGS-CELLENT TIME.

BLOX TIP

Don't avoid falling in the sea—in fact, dive right in! There are lots of items to collect and red coins to harvest, making this a great place if you want to grind for coins.

By Whacky Wizards

5 WACKY WIZARDS

In some ways this is a regular quest-based game that requires you to complete tasks in order to locate items. The fun—and weird—bit comes when you put those things into a cauldron and make a potion, often with absurd effects. Some of the potions are useful, like the ones that give you a speed boost. Some are not, such as those that transform you into a Bored Ape NFT or make you explode.

Wacky Wizards takes place in an open arena where you can mingle with other players and give potions to each other so you can try out the effects—making it a nice social experience, too.

WHAT WILL THESE WACKY WIZARDS DO NEXT?

BLOX TIP

Flying is a handy ability to acquire early—make the Mermaid Potion by using the Fairy (a starter ingredient) and the Fish, which is in a passage at the bottom of the lake.

By lick.io

4 DEVIOUS LICK SIMULATOR

The Devious Lick meme involves stealing things from schools, and obviously we would not encourage you to do such a thing. Instead we'd encourage you to play *Devious Lick Simulator.* As the name suggests, it mimics the experience.

You run around a school harvesting anything in sight—lockers, desks, clocks, soap dispensers—and selling it to buy upgrades that enable you to harvest more things . . . and so on. It's a simple, silly game, but there's something irresistible about it.

UNLOCK CUTE COMPANIONS.

BLOX TIP

When you have a full team of three pets, maximize your harvesting by using them to harvest multiple items at the same time.

By @OcculusAnubis

3 VAULT SEVEN

Vault Seven is *creepy* weird. You start the game in the middle of an abandoned facility. You wander around and explore, with no guidance on what you're actually supposed to be *doing*. There are rooms you can open, and rooms that you don't have the security clearance to enter. There is also a slice of pizza that shouts "PIZZA!!" and attacks you.

As you make your way around, you may find secrets indicating the purpose of the facility—were they really trying to discover how to travel between dimensions? And what are those glowing mineshafts about? Good luck . . .

I WONDER WHAT HAPPENS IN VAULT 8?

BLOX TIP

Since there's no map, the colored lines on the floor are very helpful—follow them until you find the sign that tells you where each one leads.

By Minimal Games

2 THE PRESENTATION EXPERIENCE

Are you the class clown? Or do you want to be, but you don't want to get into actual trouble? Then *The Presentation Experience* is for you. Players sit in a classroom and take turns giving a lecture on whatever random topic appears on the blackboard. Then everyone else disrupts the presentation in a variety of ways, spending points to do so.

LET ME TELL YOU SOMETHING . . .

This game is the ultimate in dumb fun. You can try to be funny in your presentation and get a higher grade from your classmates, and maybe even distract them long enough to stop them from shouting memes like "EMOTIONAL DAMAGE!!" at you. But probably not. Whatever approach you choose, it's a great place to blow off some steam.

BLOX TIP

You can earn double points while playing on a private server. Invite your friends!

By First Church of Bubbleism

1 PURPLE SKITTLES

Purple Skittles is an adventure game where you play as a thing called Timothy and must traverse an odd landscape where your path is frequently blocked by snakemen who live in shoes and such. To get past them, you must beat them at air hockey. Your ultimate goal is to find eight purple Skittles.

That doesn't even begin to describe the unique weirdness of *Purple Skittles.* We love this game. The dialogue, which appears in 8-bit-style boxes when you talk to a character, is really funny—you want to keep going just to meet new characters and have new conversations. The air hockey is pretty challenging but very well rendered—stick with it, and you'll get good!

WHAT'S YOUR FAVE COLOR?

BLOX TIP

Bounce the air hockey puck off the sides of the table—a straight shot will likely be blocked easily by your opponent.

WEIRD GAMES QUIZ

The parrots in *Dancing Parrots* are similar to those in what other game?

What badge can you earn in *Survive Ariana Grande in Area 51*?

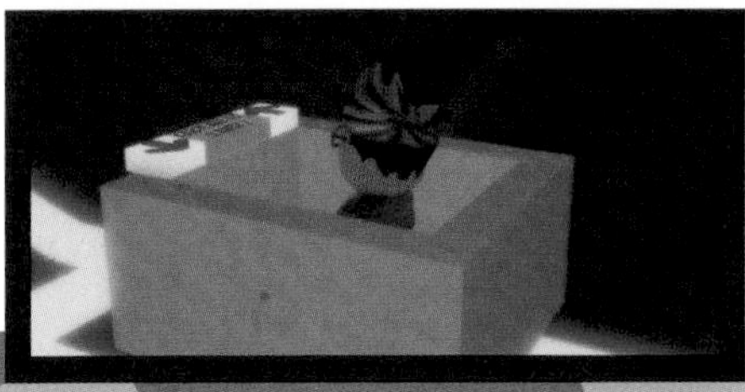

What mode straightens your neck in *Human Giraffe?*

What are the enemies called in *Mega Noob Simulator*?

How many keys are there to find in *Eg!*?

What kind of potion is made by combining the Fairy and the Fish in *Wacky Wizards*?

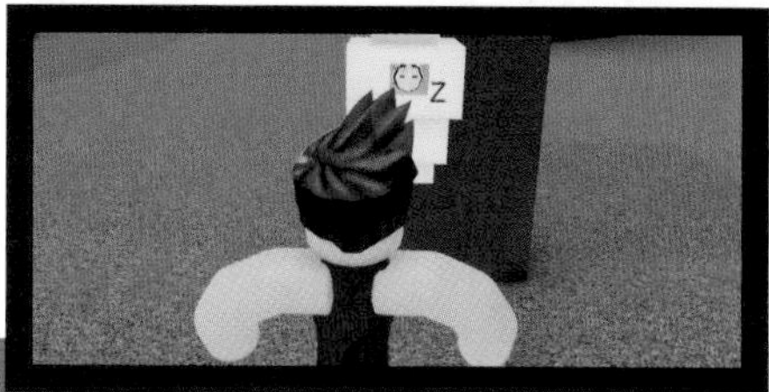

How many pets make up a full team in *Devious Lick Simulator*?

What type of food attacks you in *Vault Seven*?

Name a meme you can shout in *The Presentation Experience*.

Who is the hero of *Purple Skittles*?

HORROR GAMES

Horror games are huge on Roblox. Whether you want creepy mysteries, battles with monsters, or all-out survival action, there's a game for you. In fact, there are lots!

HORROR GAMES

Despite its bright, blocky graphics, Roblox is weirdly well suited to creepy experiences.

STAY PUT

A *lot* of horror games on Roblox are about exploring a deserted haunted house. There's a simple reason for this—it's easier to program a game that doesn't have a lot of moving elements or combat systems, and the designer can just focus on putting the environment and the puzzle elements together.

STAY ALIVE

There are also murderer games, which make good use of Roblox's multiplayer system. These will be familiar to anyone who's played *Among Us*—one or more players are randomly assigned the role of murderer, and the other players have to avoid getting killed by them. A lot of Roblox murderer games use a system where only one player can stop the murderer, and the others just have to survive.

ONE ROUND AT A TIME

Then there are straight-up survival games, where the threat comes from NPCs—the player is thrown into a dangerous situation and just has to come through it. There'll usually be rounds, with each one bringing a new wave of enemies or a new environment to survive.

WARNING!

Exercise caution when playing this type of game. Many of them aren't especially scary, and we've picked ones we think are suitable for younger players. But there are definitely some unsuitable games out there!

By Digital Destruction

10 INSANE ELEVATOR!

This is a good game for a quick play, and it starts when you and a group of other players board an elevator. The elevator moves between different floors, each of which has a different horror experience on it, which you must try to survive. Complete the challenge by surviving all the floors!

Despite drawing on classic scary scenarios, this game is more silly than scary. You all run around and try to avoid getting bloxxed. The power-ups you can buy with your earnings do help you clear the levels, so always visit the shop whenever you get pinged back to the lobby.

THIS GAME IS NO JOKE!

BLOX TIP

Don't go down corridors just for the sake of it—staying still and waiting for the monster to appear is generally a better tactic.

By PANDEMIC.

9 ZOMBIE BLITZ

Roblox has lots of zombie games, but this is one of the best, offering classic zombie-slaying action. Blitz HQ is under attack from waves of zombies, and it's your job to kill them. That's basically it!

Zombie Blitz is a first-person shooter with a straightforward game mechanic. The more waves of zombies you destroy, the more money you get, which enables you to buy better weapons . . . you get the idea. Up to eight players can share an arena, making this a great game to play with friends.

BLITZ THOSE ZOMBIES!

BLOX TIP

Go and buy the boosts to your reload speed, stamina, and headshot damage as quickly as you can—they're not expensive, and they really help you survive longer.

By Hot Cake Games

8 NIGHTMARES

A similar concept to *Insane Elevator!*, *Nightmares* puts a group of players into a mansion and then subjects them to a series of "nightmares." The scenarios vary—sometimes you're in a warzone, sometimes a zombie apocalypse, sometimes being chased by a monstrous SpongeBob—but the task is always the same . . . to survive!

SSSSSURVIVAL IS ALL THAT COUNTS!

It's fun that you never quite know what's coming next, like a horror version of *Fall Guys*, and it adds an extra challenge. You can't just play one round over and over to work out your tactics, you just have to take them as they come.

BLOX TIP

If you're playing on a PC, this is one of those Roblox games that's much better with a mouse, since you need it to use weapons!

By BDStudios

7 GEISHA

To stand out among all the haunted house games on Roblox, the environment has to be brilliant—and this is what makes *Geisha* a winner. The traditional Japanese buildings you move through look great and get the most out of the Roblox graphics system.

The gameplay—partly inspired by the Japanese urban legend Teke Teke—involves searching for keys and avoiding the hostile spirit that stalks the house, with some very effective jumpscares. The puzzles are pretty straightforward to begin with, but as the game goes on you'll be desperate to solve them before you're found!

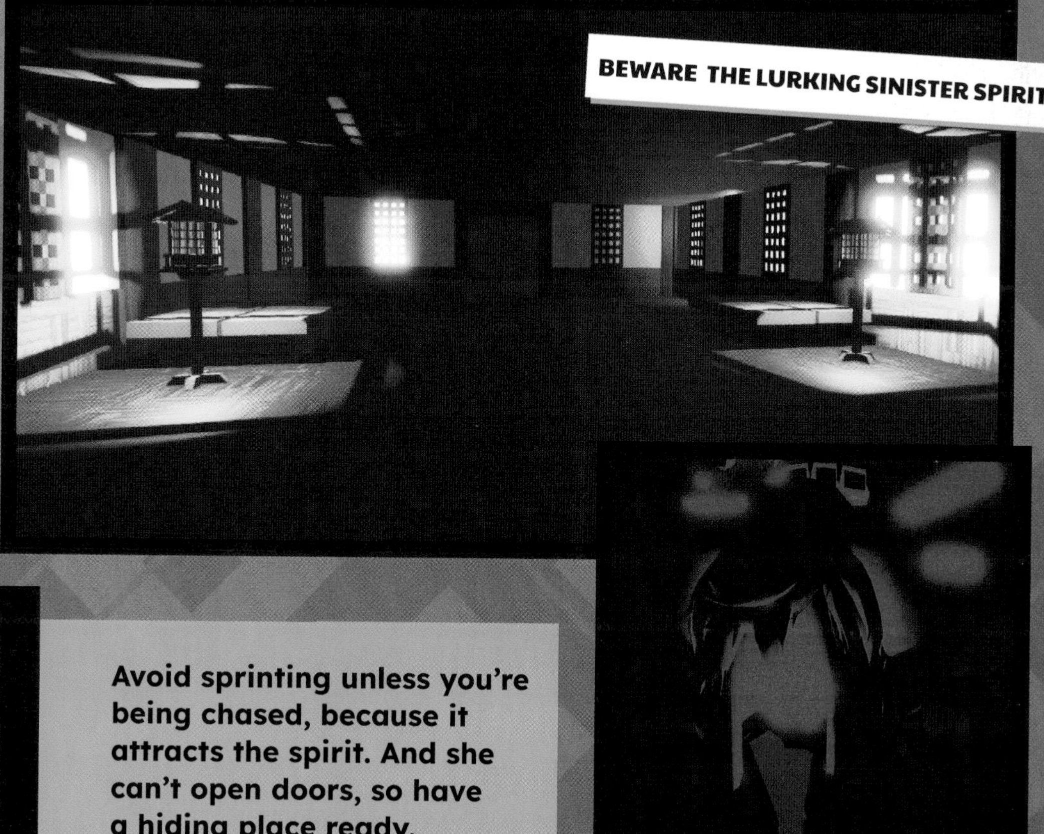

BEWARE THE LURKING SINISTER SPIRIT.

BLOX TIP

Avoid sprinting unless you're being chased, because it attracts the spirit. And she can't open doors, so have a hiding place ready.

By Otter Space

6 A WOLF OR OTHER

A Wolf or Other—the initials spell *AWOO*—uses a classic scenario. A group of villagers know that a wolf is among them, but they don't know who it is. One of you gets to be the werewolf, another gets to be the hunter—and the rest of you just have to survive!

The environment, which is vaguely 17th-century, is pretty great, and it's really enhanced by the fact that you're assigned a character, rather than just playing as your usual Robloxian self. Getting to know the map is essential, so give it a few plays!

A HOWL LOT OF FUN!

BLOX TIP

If you're the wolf, use your howl to locate the villagers and stop them from hiding in cupboards!

By @ojbaby

5 FINDERS KEEPERS

Another haunted-house game, *Finders Keepers* uses a first-person perspective as you play a paranormal investigator trapped in a house by an unknown entity. It's up to you to search the house for discs that will play in the laptop and reveal parts of the mystery around the house.

This game really works because of the thought and attention that's gone into the environment and story. The house is filled with cupboards and drawers you can open as you hunt for clues, making it one of the most immersive games on Roblox.

HOPE YOU AREN'T SCARED OF THE DARK!

BLOX TIP

After playing the first disc and hearing the noise, head for the door that's next to a blue sofa, to the right of a locked door to the outside. It'll open if you stand behind the sofa.

By @bobulator

4 THE HAUNTED IMPERIAL HOTEL

What's creepier than a haunted house? A haunted hotel! *The Haunted Imperial Hotel* is a terrific idea for a Roblox game, and it's been done really well. You wander the corridors of this partly wrecked hotel, abandoned after an earthquake on Halloween 2009, and try to uncover its secrets.

MAYBE RETHINK YOUR VAYCAY PLANS.

The scale of the playing area, and the obstacles you have to get past to move around it, create much of the game's creepy atmosphere—it's really hard not to get lost, you get turned around so often. But there's no other way—you have to surrender yourself to the hotel . . .

BLOX TIP

If you go up the steps to the first floor near the reception desk, then go through the first open door on the left, you can fall through to the basement and explore that.

By @Kinnis97

3 STOP IT, SLENDER!

Stop It, Slender! is a murderer game with a twist. At the start of each round, one of the players is randomly chosen to be Slenderman, a creature who drains you of energy if you look at him. If you look at him for too long, you die. There's no mystery about which of you is Slender—but the other players can't *see* Slender until he chooses to be visible.

Meanwhile, the other players must try to collect eight hidden pages from a dark and creepy environment, activating generators to open up new areas, before Slender gets them all or the time runs out. It's really fun and addictive stuff, whichever side you're on.

DON'T LOOK AT SLENDER.

BLOX TIP

When you get a choice of maps, don't choose the Complex unless you like a challenge—it's very hard to find all the pages there!

By @Polyhex

2 SUPER BOMB SURVIVAL

Definitely in the "survival" category rather than "horror," *Super Bomb Survival* is simple yet brilliant. A bunch of players are dropped into a small map. Bombs appear and missiles fall, damaging players and destroying parts of the environment. You must survive as long as you can—and you can help or hinder other players!

BOMBS AWAY!

This idea is so well suited to Roblox, and there's enough variety in the maps and gameplay to keep you coming back. Credit, too, for making a really fun lobby—it's designed like an arcade (complete with ugly carpet), where you can choose to shop, spectate, or goof around with the cannons.

BLOX TIP

If you think you've found a safe spot and decide to just stand there while the timer winds down . . . don't! A bomb will spawn near you.

By @MiniToon

1 PIGGY

Since its launch in January 2020, *Piggy* has become one of the runaway hits of Roblox, racking up over 10 billion visits! It started life as a parody of a certain popular preschool TV series, but it's moved on to develop its own lore, introducing new characters and telling a story over multiple seasons.

One of the smartest things about *Piggy* is its choice of game modes—so it can be a murderer game where one player is the killer, or where one player is secretly a traitor, or you can choose to play against a bot. It's not an easy game—there aren't many places to hide—but players keep coming back until they crack it!

DON'T LET THE PORK CHOP YOU!

BLOX TIP

Spamming the crouch button can help you move faster through vents. Try it!

HORROR GAMES QUIZ

How do you complete the challenge of *Insane Elevator!*?

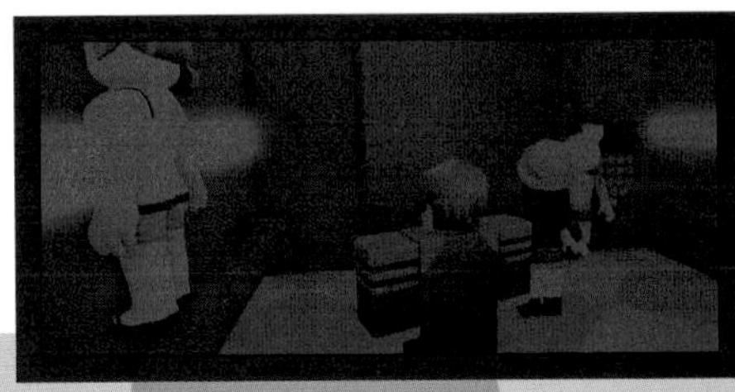

How many players can share an arena in *Zombie Blitz*?

A monstrous version of which cartoon character appears in *Nightmares*?

What Japanese urban legend was part of the inspiration for *Geisha*?

In *A Wolf or Other*, which player can kill the werewolf?

What do you have to search for in *Finders Keepers*?

What year did *The Haunted Imperial Hotel* close?

How many pages do you have to collect in a round of *Stop It, Slender!*?

Name three things you can do in the lobby of *Super Bomb Survival.*

When was *Piggy* launched?

HIDDEN GEMS

It's easy to get drawn into just playing the big Roblox games that have over a hundred million hits—but there are many, many great games that haven't had as much attention. Allow us to show you some of our favorites . . .

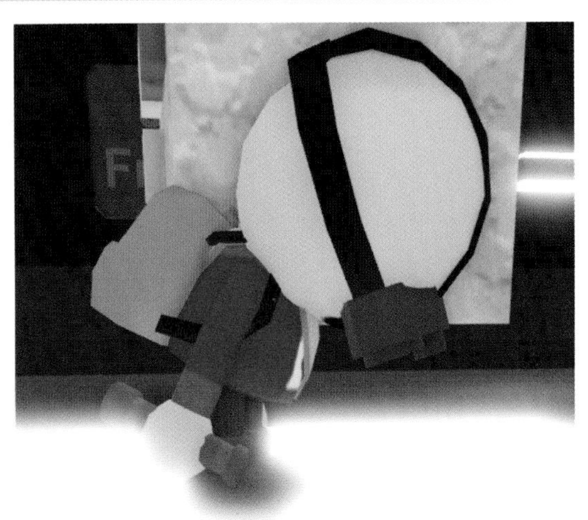

HIDDEN GEMS

All the games in this section are tried and tested, often with millions of visits—but they're ones we've not seen on the usual lists of top Roblox games. We think they deserve to be better known.

GENRE BREAKING

One thing you'll notice about a lot of these games is they offer something a bit different from the most popular games on Roblox. The biggest Roblox genres—survival, RPG, tycoon—have their own sub-fanbases, and when a game in one of those genres breaks big, those fans tend to flock to it.

THINK OUTSIDE THE BOX

There are so many other types of games on Roblox, and they don't always fit the obvious genres. Often, that's exactly what makes them interesting! It's cool to think outside the box and come up with a different experience.

TAKE YOUR TIME

Some of them are slow-burners—they might not immediately grab you as quickly as some other games, but give them time and they'll reveal new depths.

SOMETHING NEW

We're also covering some awesome games that have a very different look—games that don't use traditional Roblox avatars or graphics styles. Some of these games are really pushing what you can do with the platform, and we're very impressed!

By BRIBBLECO™

10 SUPER CUBE CAVERN

In a world that's frozen over, only the underground is safe. And, in fact, it's not *that* safe because there's tons of monsters down there. *Super Cube Cavern* is a dungeon-crawling game where the next room is generated as you go along, so it's never the same experience twice.

There's definitely an element of *Minecraft* about it, too—not just in the design of the caverns you explore, but in the way you can collect items and then craft them into new ones at crafting tables. Be careful, it can be quite unforgiving at first, when you're literally hitting enemies with an old stick you've found!

CLIMB AND EXPLORE!

BLOX TIP

The bow is a very useful item to craft, but don't waste your arrows, as they can only be obtained from chests and by killing enemies, or by buying them!

By The Kinetic Abilities

9 THE KINETIC ABILITIES

The Kinetic Abilities is a superpowered combat game. You choose a type of superpower—fire, water, air, electricity, and so on—and then drop into a random area in the (very richly designed) game environment. You then face off against other players, leveling up your powers as you go.

This can be a bit slow-moving at first, but the superpowers are very well rendered—we love how they light up the nighttime landscape—and once you unlock some of the higher powers, it gets seriously fun.

THINGS ARE HEATING UP . . .

BLOX TIP

Either drop in with a friend and you can defeat each other to level up, or go to the village where you can fight the slow-moving police.

By @vetexgames

ADVENTURE STORY!

This quest-based adventure game boasts a big open world and a turn-based combat system that is a nice change of pace from some of the more frantic combat encountered in similar games. You travel around the map talking to characters and accepting missions, increasing your standing in this world.

ADVENTURE TIME!

At first, all you can do is punch and the combat can seem a little slow, but very quickly you'll level up and acquire skills that make it more exciting—and any players can join a battle, so you can put together a party with friends or just randoms you meet in the game. This speeds things up even more, since you'll be able to deal with multiple enemies more easily.

BLOX TIP

The wallet you start off with fills up quickly, so go and spend those coins on health-giving items as soon as you get the chance.

By Yellow Gearworks

7 WITCHING HOUR

This is a survival game with a difference. It takes place in an arena inside a spooky forest called the Grimwood, and at the start of each round, each player is placed on a square over a deadly pit. Threats will appear at random—you just have to survive them!

You can hop from one square to another if you need to escape—for instance, if a bomb appears on your square—but just watch out you don't land yourself in worse trouble. A round of *Witching Hour* doesn't take long, but it's easy to get sucked into playing another, and another . . .

WELCOME TO GRIMWOOD . . .

BLOX TIP

Normally you can't jump diagonally from one square to another, but if there's a crate on the corner of your square, you can sometimes make it by jumping from the top.

By Bitsquid Games

6 HEXARIA

Another adventure game with a turn-based combat system, *Hexaria* adds a very clever game mechanic and is perhaps the best game of its type. If you've ever played *Dungeons and Dragons* using a grid to work out actions during combat, you'll see what's going on here.

The whole world is divided into hexagons, and when combat starts, a bunch of these hexagons form an arena. Your movement is based on these hexagons, while your actions are dictated by a deck of virtual cards that appears during combat. As the game goes on, you can collect more cards and expand your range!

ONE HEXAGON AT A TIME.

BLOX TIP

After the tutorial, you'll spawn on a land with three paths. The one on the left-hand side is recommended for new players, because the other two take you to Elite Bandits.

By Slam Dunc Studios

5 DATABRAWL

It's always great to see a Roblox game with a really original look and concept, and *Databrawl* has that in spades. It looks completely different from the standard Roblox graphics style. The idea is that you're in a computer, and you can choose to play as a Program or Firewall defending the computer, or as a Virus or Malware attacking it.

From there it's your usual combat system with weapons to equip and items to collect—but it's such a fun world to spend time in, with its brightly colored retro cityscape, that you'll keep coming back.

DEBUG YOUR DATA!

BLOX TIP

Like many Roblox combat games, this one uses a point-and-click system for projectiles—much easier to use with a mouse than a trackpad.

By Century Explorers

4 BOT CLASH

Is this the cutest combat game on Roblox? In *Bot Clash* you acquire a squad of four little robots and send them out to destroy things, which earns you coins that you can use to buy more robots via a gacha system. You can also turn your robots into upgrade materials when you no longer need them.

The gameplay is simple and doesn't change much from one area to the next. But it's weirdly addictive all the same, as you unlock upgrades and new types of robots. And the design is terrific!

THE ULTIMATE CLASH OF BOTS.

BLOX TIP

Save some gems for the mount upgrades in the Space Station—you can make your mount's attack much, much more effective.

By Stealthy Entertainment

3 STEALTH 2

Basically this is a Roblox version of *Assassin's Creed*, and it has a small but avid following. You play as an assassin who has to carry out missions while being as stealthy as possible, using parkour and the various tools at your disposal (for instance, you can pull up your hood to make it less likely you'll be noticed).

It's very smartly put together, with a lot more controls and options than your average Roblox game. This means it can take a little while to get the hang of it all, but it's also got more depth than other games, with a world that really draws you in.

DON'T LET THEM SEE YOU COMING . . .

BLOX TIP

When using sixth sense to find a person, you'll need to do some legwork. The objective will have a larger icon above their head, which will hang around longer than the other things highlighted with sixth sense.

By nextReality Games

2 JOURNEY TO THE SUN

Journey to the Sun has a similar vibe to *Journey*—maybe that influenced the title—but it's got a distinct Roblox twist. You travel around the Grand Nexus (which has been frozen in time), as the Angel's Chosen, a character who can leap high and long distances, searching for Sacred Flames.

You'll quickly realize this is actually a parkour game, so instead of fighting enemies, you have to explore by using timed jumps and finding the best route. But the huge, fantastic landscape and the characters you speak to along the way add an extra dimension to the experience.

LET THE SUN SHINE.

BLOX TIP

With some of the narrower ledges, angle the camera so you're looking straight down and use your shadow to see where you're going to land.

By @Pulsarnova

1 SPACE SAILORS

Space Sailors is a (fairly) realistic space-travel sim, in which the player can pilot a rocket into Earth's orbit, dock with the International Space Station, travel to the Moon—or go even farther.

The detail is incredible and quite possibly the best graphics you'll find anywhere on Roblox, and it's very cleverly programmed, too. We're not even sure *how* they made the rocket go through its stages of flight or created the effect of traveling such great distances. It's brilliantly done and is a great social experience, too. This is what Roblox can do!

GET INTO ORBIT!

BLOX TIP

When you're in zero gravity on the ISS, PC users need to use the "W" and "S" buttons on the keyboard to move and the right mouse button to change direction.

HIDDEN GEMS QUIZ

1 What's happened to the surface of the world in *Super Cube Cavern*?

2 Name two superpowers in *The Kinetic Abilities*.

3 What's the only combat move you start off with in *Adventure Story*?

4 What's the forest called in *Witching Hour*?

What do you need to acquire in *Hexaria* to get new actions?

What are the two groups attacking the computer in *Databrawl*?

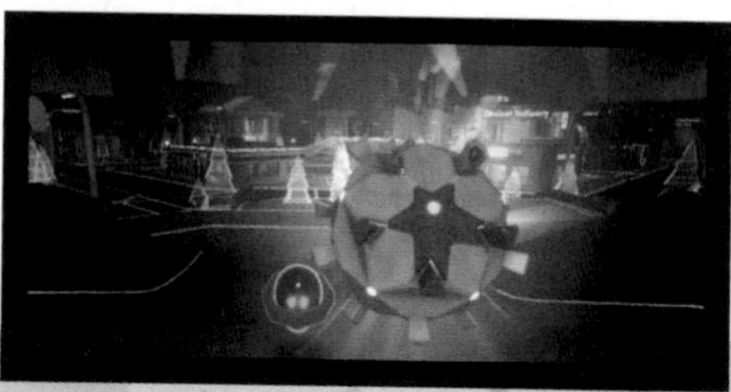

7

How many robots make up a squad in *Bot Clash*?

8

How can you avoid being noticed in *Stealth 2*?

9

Who do you play as in *Journey to the Sun*?

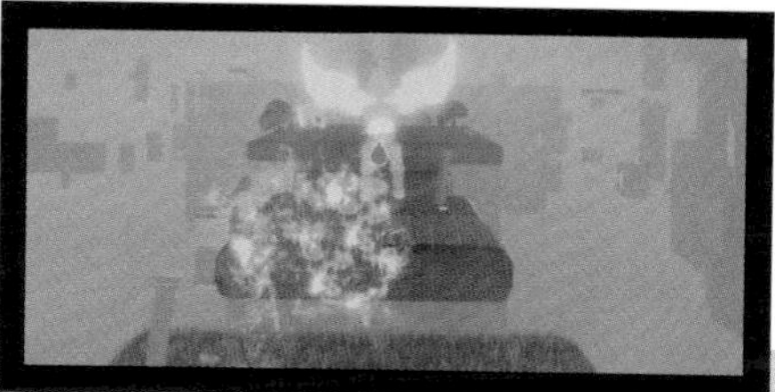

10

Where can you dock in *Space Sailors*?

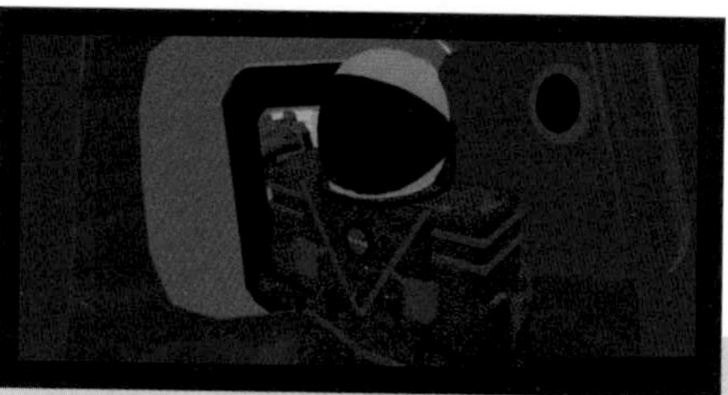

BUILDING BETTER GAMES

The great thing about Roblox is that anyone can make a game! Roblox Studio gives you everything you need to make your own game in about half an hour. But there's far, far more you can do, and in time you can master the techniques to make your game ideas a reality!

If you want to make your own Roblox games, the first thing you need is Roblox Studio—which is available for Windows and Mac, and is free!

Go to **https://www.roblox.com/create** and download it.

THE HARDWARE

As with Roblox itself, you'll find Roblox Studio runs much more smoothly on a decent gaming machine that can handle the graphics. A good video card and a 1.6 GHz processor (or faster) will help a lot, and ideally your machine should be less than five years old if it's a desktop computer—or three years if it's a laptop.

CHECK YOUR SPECS

We also recommend you use a PC that uses Windows 10 or higher, or a Mac with OS 10.11 or above. Roblox Studio will run on lower-spec computers, but it'll probably be slow, so you might need some patience!

SAVE SPACE

You'll also need at least 1 GB of memory to install the Studio, as well as space to save your projects. You can also save projects to your Roblox account—which requires a good broadband connection, but if you're a Roblox player, we figure you already have that.

BLOX TIP

If you're using a laptop, you may just have a trackpad rather than a separate mouse. We suggest picking up a two-button mouse with a scroll wheel—it'll make a lot of things much quicker.

BUILDING BETTER

1 Open up the Studio and you'll see different **game templates.** Open one of the templates and you'll see a *lot* of different options—you can put objects into your game and change their sizes, alter the terrain, change the game settings, and much, much more!

2 So what kind of game do you want to make? The great thing about Roblox is it offers such wide possibilities, your game can be as big or as small as you like . . . but while you're still learning how to use it, maybe start small.

3 If you've never made a game before, we suggest starting with a **Line Runner** game. There's a template for them in Studio—select it and you'll see a baseplate with nine segments on it.

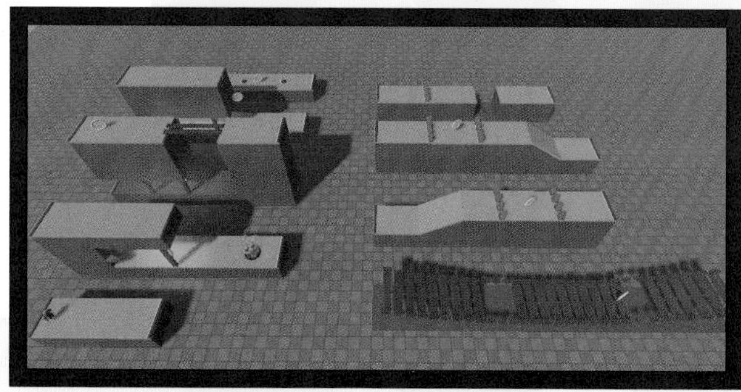

4 When anyone plays your Line Runner game, these segments will be put together in a random order. You can play around with the segments, change their colors, surfaces, put NPCs on them . . . do whatever you want to make it your own.

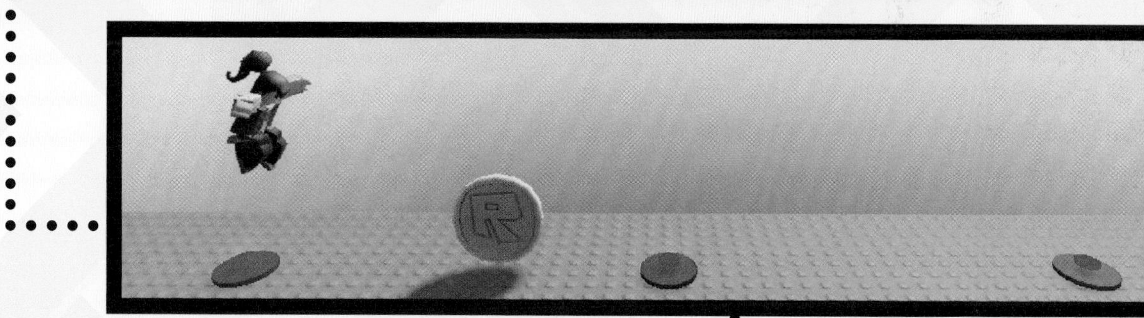

5 A Line Runner game isn't going to set Roblox on fire, but it's a good way to start exploring the Studio—and get the satisfaction of making your first game.

6 Once you've done this, maybe move on to building an **Infinite Runner** game—these are similar to Line Runner games, but instead of viewing the action from the side, you view it from behind your character.

7 Roblox's Runner games don't involve making any **scripts**, which is helpful for newcomers. Scripts are little pieces of code that run the game. For instance, if you have a treasure chest in a game, you need scripts to make it open when the player interacts with it—and scripts that say what's inside.

8 The Runner games do use scripts, because all games do—but the scripts are already programmed into the templates.

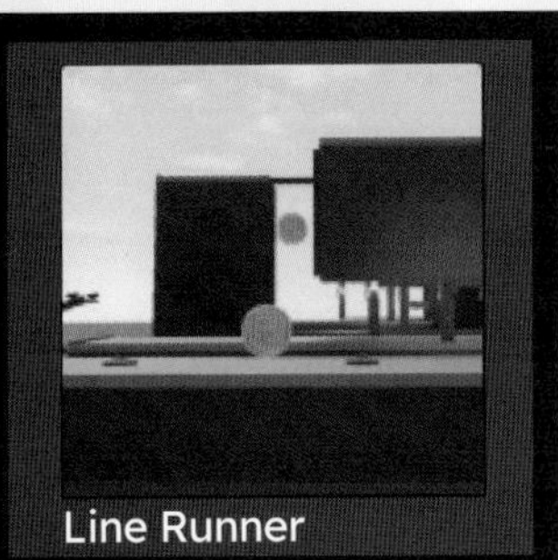

Line Runner

9 The next type of game to try if you're new to making Roblox games is an **Obby.** These use very few scripts—the main thing they need is gravity, and that's already programmed into the game environment.

Obby

10 You can build an Obby just by putting shapes into a void for players to jump between—and they can look like anything, so you can have fun designing it all. You can open up the Obby template and change whatever you like—or remove blocks entirely.

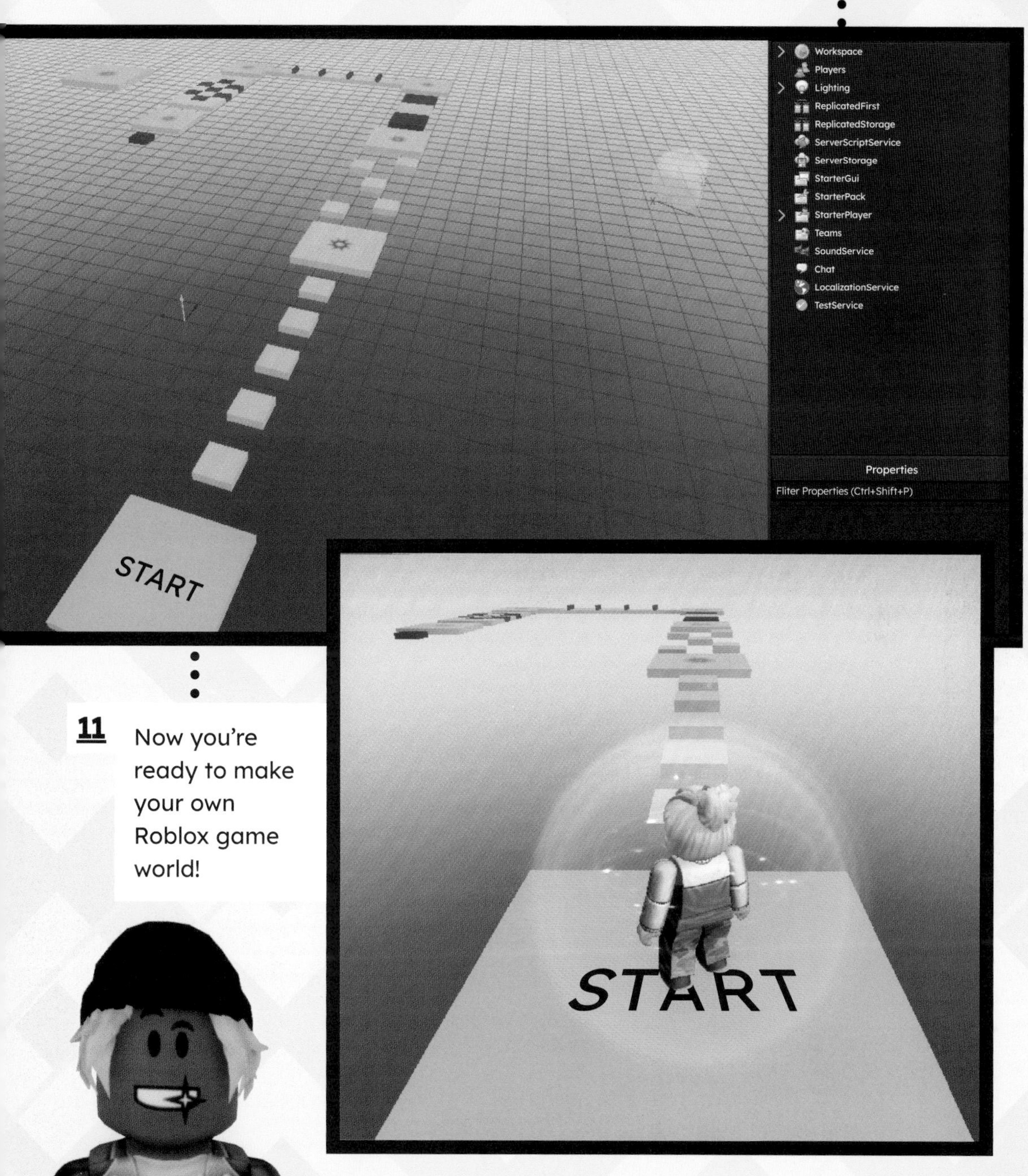

11 Now you're ready to make your own Roblox game world!

GROUNDWORK

Feeling ground down by trying to make better terrain? Try our tips . . .

1 **Terrain** in Roblox means the land your game takes place on. You can just use one of the standard terrains and build on that—but what if you want something a little different?

2 First, go to the Home tab and click on the green hills to bring up the **Terrain Editor.** There are three different categories—**Create, Region,** and **Edit.**

Editor
Terrain

Terrain Editor
Create Region Edit
Generate Import Clear

CREATE TAB

3 The **Create tab** is the quickest way to build terrain—it lets you set parameters, like the size, and features to include or exclude, such as water, mountains, or canyons. Then Studio will generate the terrain randomly, like how *Minecraft* generates a world at the start of a new game.

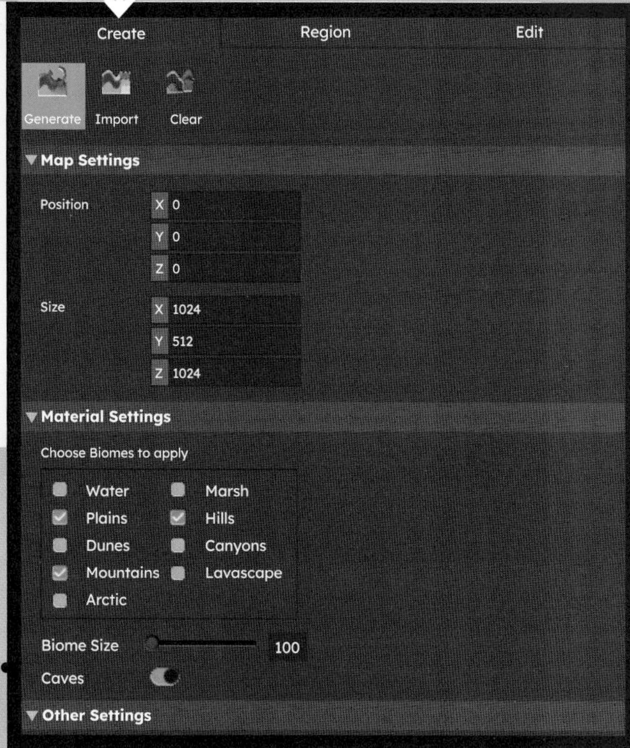

4 But if you want to design your terrain exactly how you want it, use Region and Edit.

REGION TAB

EDIT TAB

5

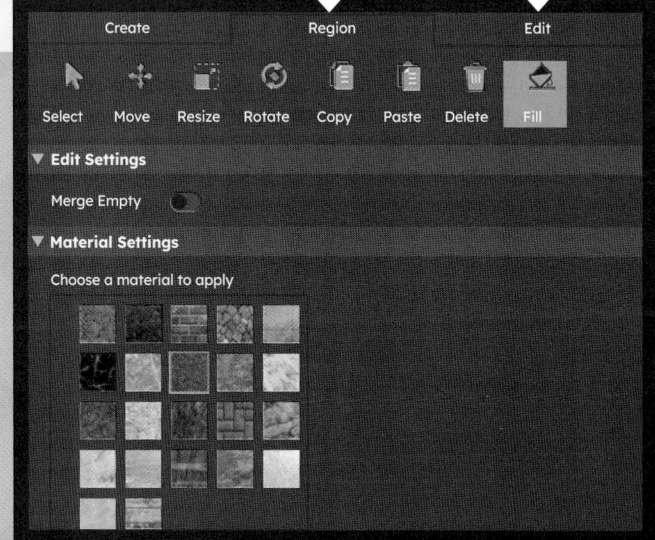

Go to **Region** first. You can use this to select one area of terrain, then change its size, move it, rotate it, or copy and paste it. And you can use **Fill** to select an area and fill it with any material. So let's start off by using Fill to make a flat slab of terrain you can work with.

BLOX TIP

Make your slab nice and deep. You may start off thinking you're only going to build upward, but if you need to dig down later, you'll need something to dig into!

6 Before clicking Fill, you'll need to choose a **material**. But what if none of the options are quite what you want? Let's say you want grass that looks dried out.

7 Go to View, and at the top of the **Explorer window,** expand Workspace and click Terrain. This will bring up all the base colors of the different terrain types. Go into Grass and change it to a straw-like yellow.

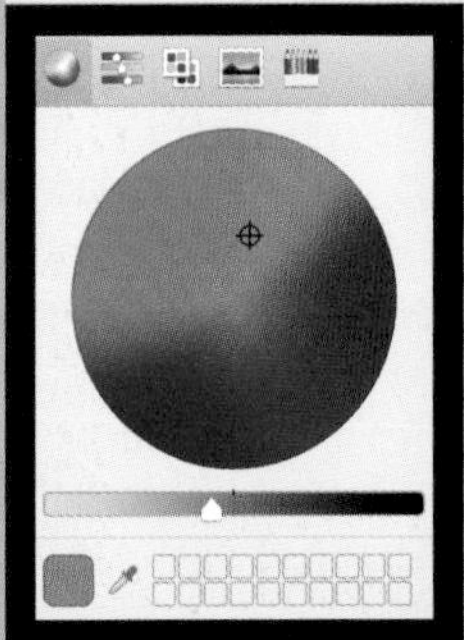

8 And there you go! All your grass will now be that color. With a few simple changes, you can really make your terrain look fresh and different. Bear in mind, though, if you change the properties of any type of terrain, *all* the terrain of that type in your environment will change. You can't have one patch of grass that's one color and one patch that's another color.

9 What you *can* do is use similar terrain types and change their settings. So by combining Grass, Ground, and Leafy Grass, and setting them to different shades of green, you can really customize your landscape.

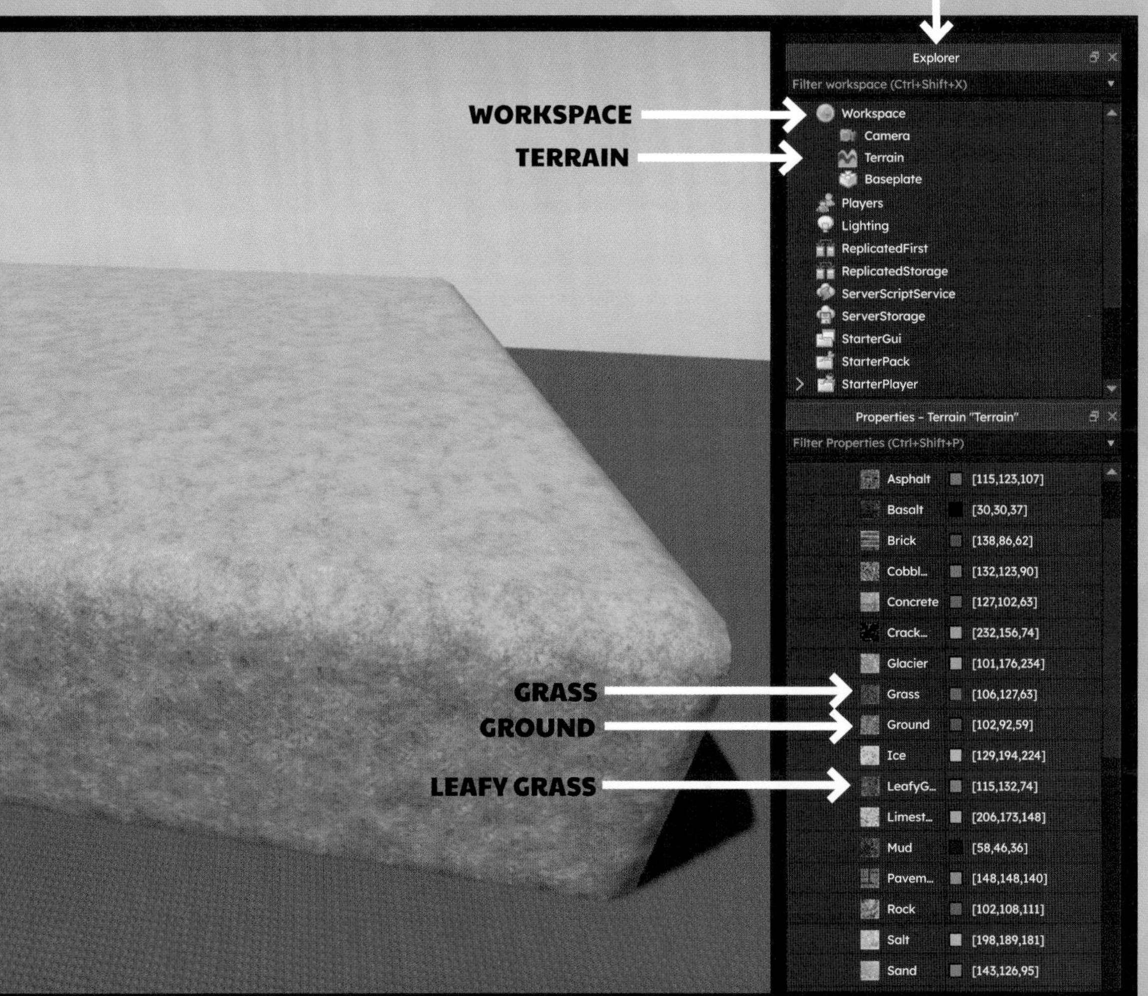

10 Now go to the **Edit tab.** The basic tools here are **Add** and **Subtract.** Click Add and you'll see a grid appear in the game creation window: This changes angle depending on how you move the camera.

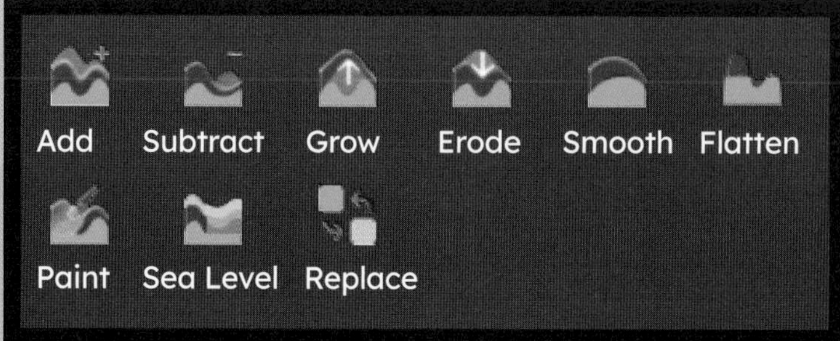

11 Using the grid takes a little getting used to, but it's really helpful when you're building in a 3D space on a 2D screen! It shows you where any new terrain you add will go. **Brush Settings** lets you change the brush shape and alter its size.

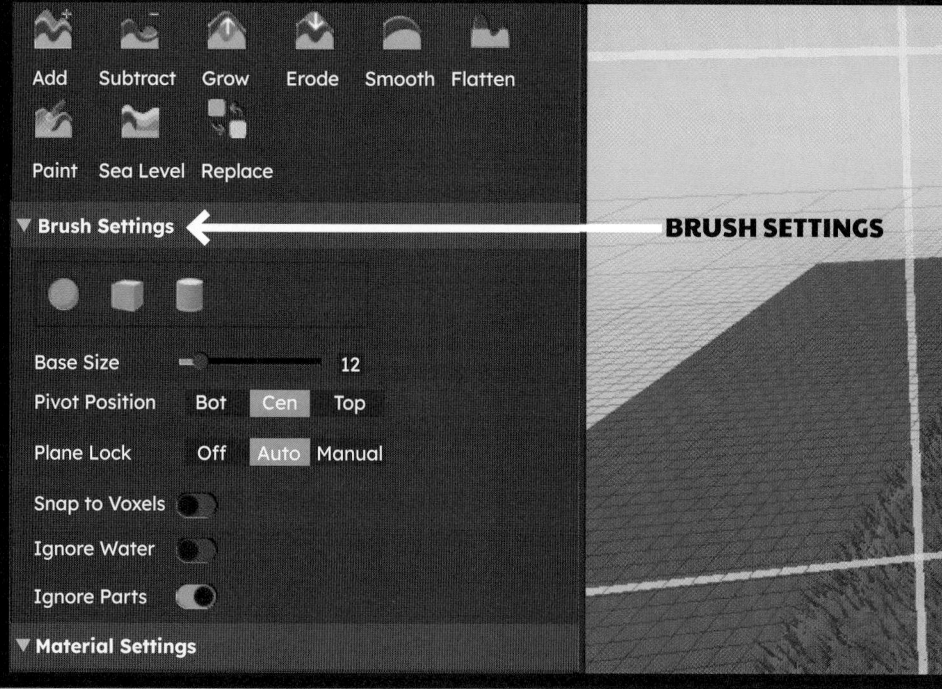

12 **Grow** will raise the terrain around your brush—the longer you click, the more the terrain grows. **Erode** pushes down the terrain. It's really easy to overdo it with these tools and end up with weird globs of terrain, so experiment with the **Strength setting** to make them work more gently.

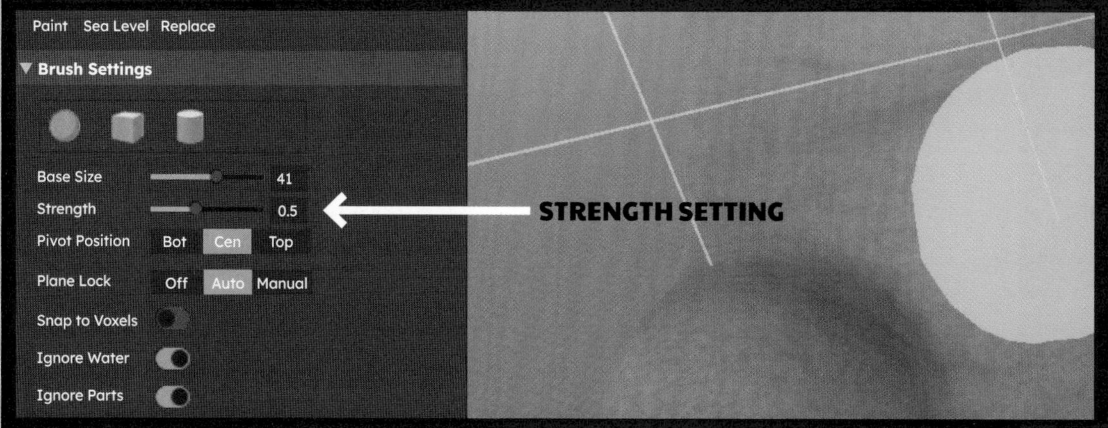

13 The **Smooth tool** is similar to Erode, but rather than getting rid of terrain completely, it just gets rid of the uneven parts and makes it look more natural.

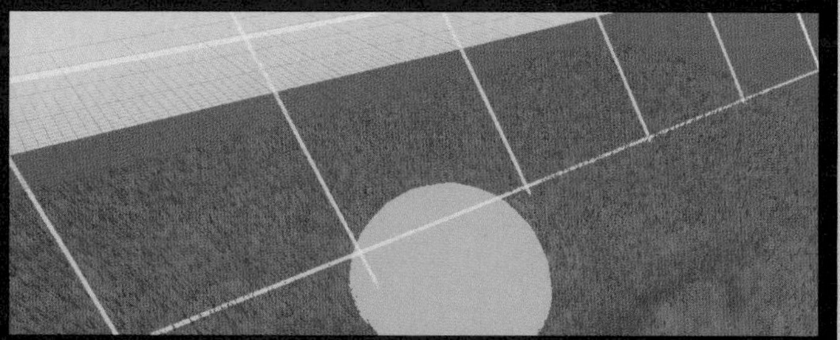

BLOX TIP

When working with a flat slab, it's a good idea to go over it and lightly use Grow and Erode to give it some texture. Once you've gotten rid of that unnatural flatness, then you can really start to model your landscape.

BLOX TIP

Remember, when making terrain, the undo button (in the top left) is your friend!

14 The **Flatten tool** sets any area of terrain to the same level—you'll notice the grid will always be horizontal when using this. There are three Flatten settings—one means the terrain is lowered to the selected level, one means it's raised, and one does both at once.

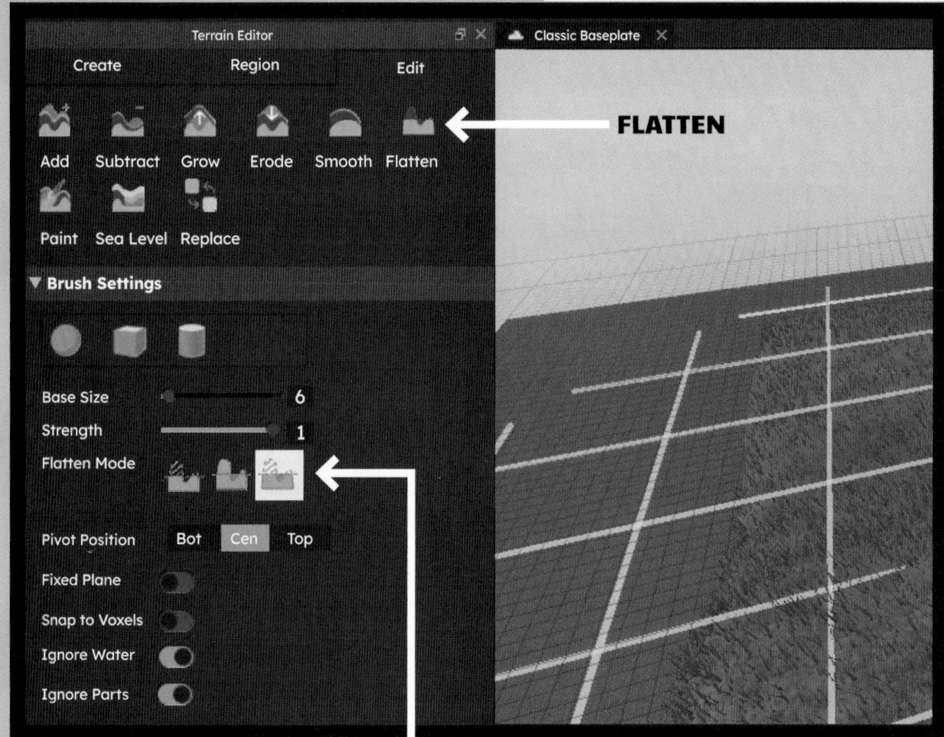

15 A mix of materials will make your terrain look much richer and more interesting—but we suggest you stick to your base material until you've gotten the basic shape together, because you can use the **Paint tool** to change any material. You don't have to build new material over the top of the old one.

16 For instance, if you want to add a path to a landscape, don't put it in at the beginning—you might find you need to change its route once you've put other parts of the landscape in.

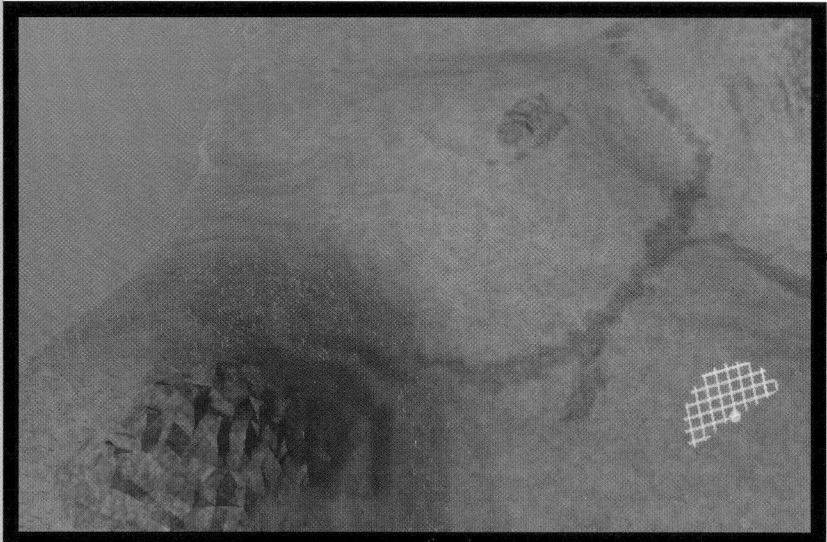

17 Some changes work better if you do build new material over the top, but do it carefully. When adding detail to terrain, making your brush smaller and turning the strength down can be a good idea. Try adding patches of bare rock to a hillside by using the Grow tool to add a light layer over the top.

THE OBJECT OF THE GAME

You've got your landscape, now you need to put stuff in it! Follow our construction course . . .

1 You can fill your landscape with stuff from the **Toolbox** (on the Home tab)—there are so many things you can find in there, from log cabins and roads to item spawners and weapons. There's even a branch of McDonald's!

2 For some items, the Toolbox is probably the way to go, especially for something tricky like a tree. Some of them even have scripts built in so they work as soon as you put them down.

3 The first thing to learn is how to put down a basic shape and make changes to it. The options you're given are **Block, Sphere, Wedge, Corner Wedge,** and **Cylinder**. It's best to start off with a block, because you can make a lot of things by putting different-sized blocks together.

4

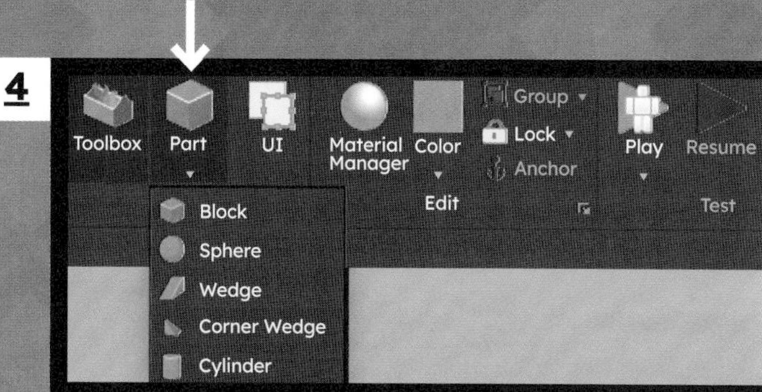

Make sure you've got your game open in Roblox Studio—or just open up a new flat terrain template if you want to practice. Go to **Part** and insert a block.

5

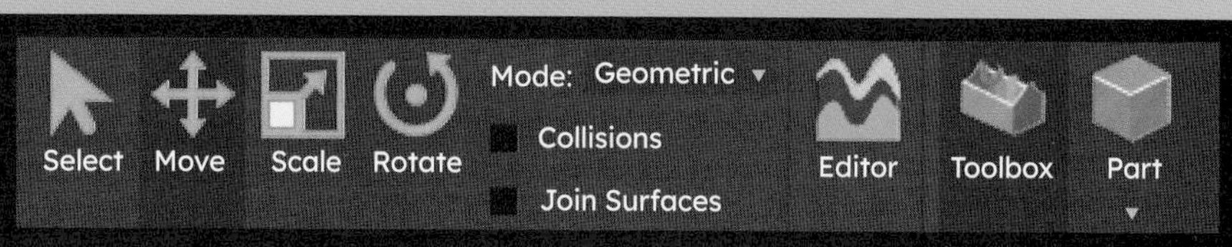

Now go to the **Select, Move, Scale,** and **Rotate** controls. When you select a part, you can grab it and move it—but you can be more precise by using the Move function.

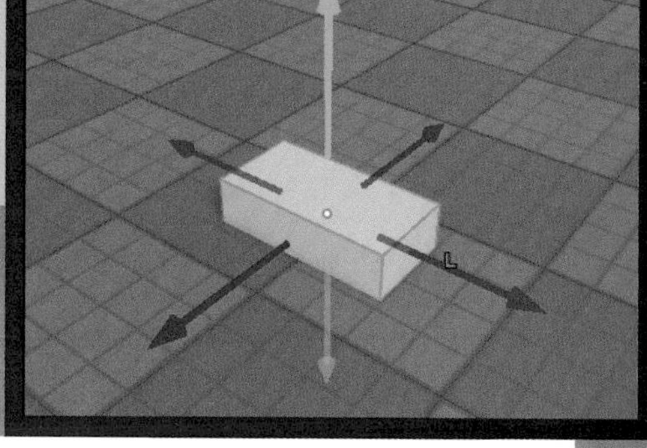

6 In Move, instead of grabbing the part, you need to click on one of the arrows. Similarly, when you select Rotate you'll see three different loops—click on one of them to rotate the part in that direction.

7 The most important control is Scale, because this doesn't just change the size of the block—it lets you change any of its dimensions. Click on any of the colored dots to make your block longer or shorter in any direction—make it thinner to create a wall or floor.

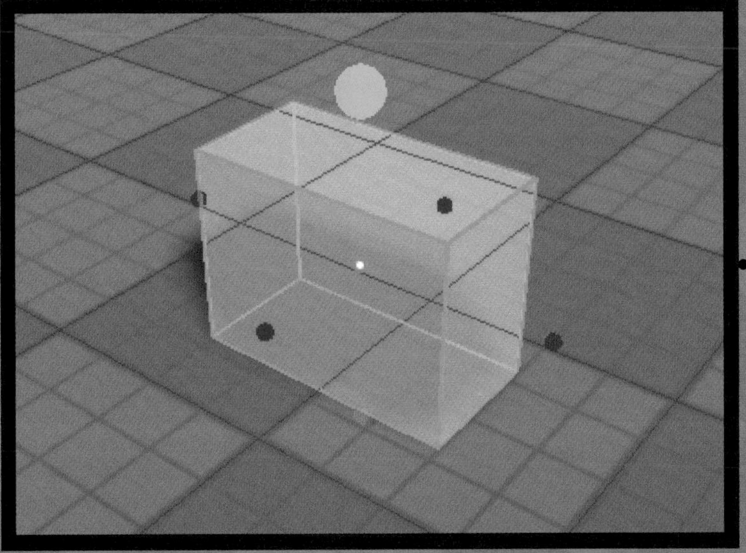

8 *But wait*—you may be thinking as you adjust your blocks—*I've seen Roblox models with thinner blocks than that, and with blocks tilted at different angles, too. How'd they do that?*

9 The answer is on the **Model tab,** on the box marked Snap to Grid.

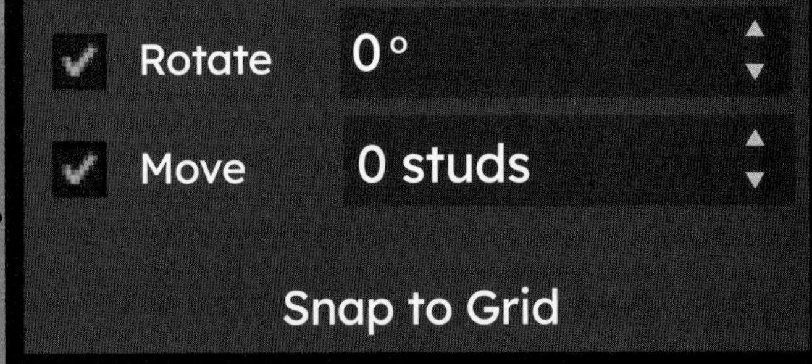

10 The default rotation is 45 degrees, which means you can make a part horizontal, vertical, or a diagonal in between. Try changing this to 15 degrees—you'll suddenly find there are lots of other positions. You can even reduce it to zero degrees and have totally smooth movement.

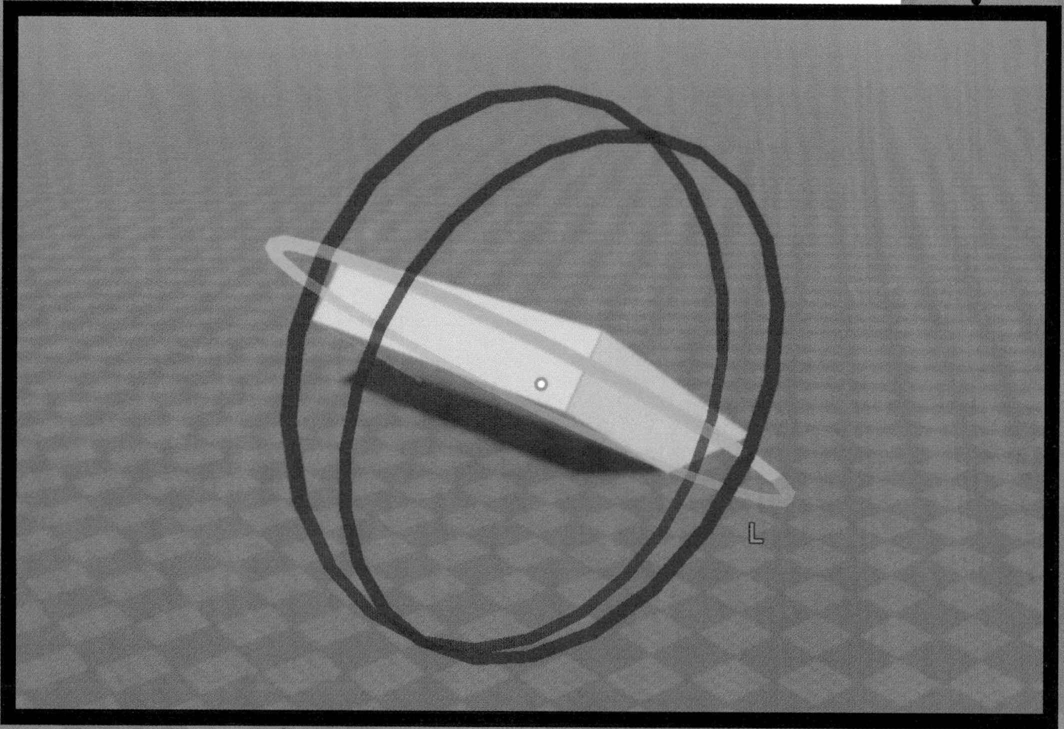

11 And you can change the movement to place parts more precisely. The default is one stud, so try setting it to 0.2. Again, setting it to zero will make the movement completely smooth.

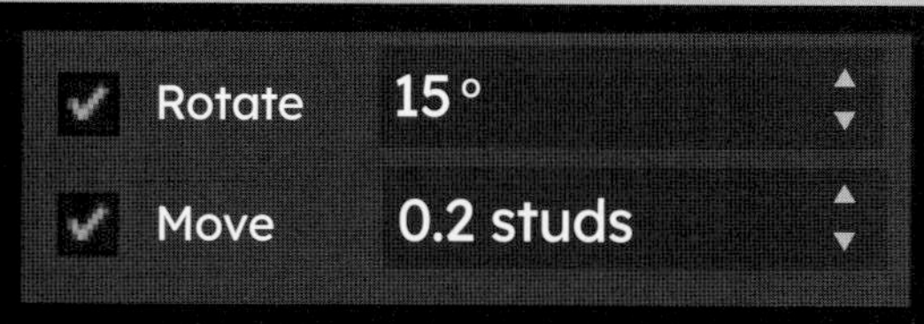

12 If you want to take advantage of these features, we suggest setting these numbers to 15 degrees rotation and 0.1 or 0.2 movement. These should be enough to give you more freedom. You'll find this also enables you to make thinner blocks—very useful for walls and roofs.

13 You can change the color of any part—the options for this are up top, under **Edit.** However, if the exact color you want isn't on the palate, go into the Explorer window and make sure the part you're working with is highlighted.

14 Look down at the **Properties** window, and you'll find a full range of colors there. If you want to use a color again, save it to your custom colors palate—it's much easier than trying to match the exact color from the huge range available.

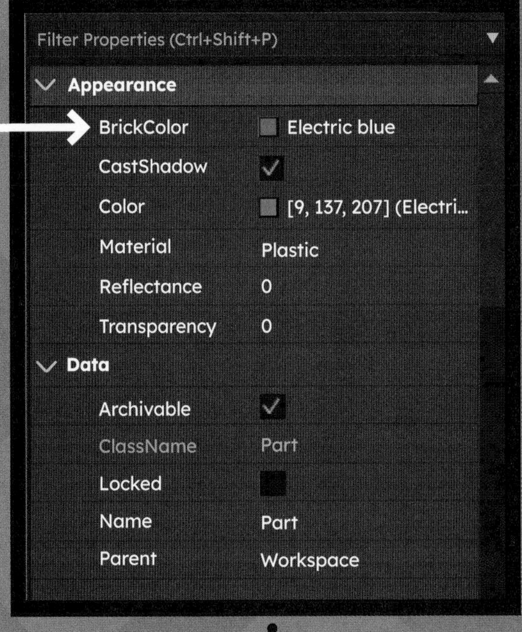

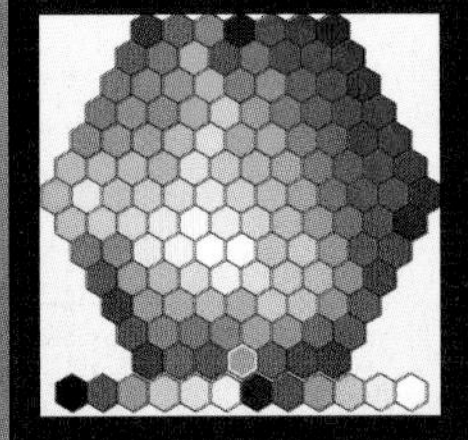

15 And if you want something different in terms of material, you can find lots of alternatives in the Toolbox. Just search for "materials," and you'll find **texture packs.** These often take the form of a whole load of small blocks with different patterns on the surface.

16 Look at the texture pack in the Explorer window, and you'll see each block listed. Click on any of these blocks in the Explorer window, and you'll see the texture it has.

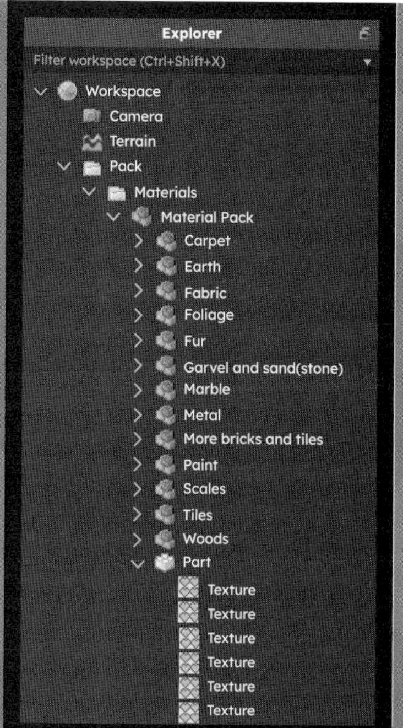

17 Right-click and copy the texture you want, then go back over to whatever you're building and click on the part you want to change. Right-click and choose "paste into." This should give it the new texture! Once you're done, you can get rid of the blocks from the texture pack.

18 We recommend you experiment with these colors and materials, and use a range of them in your creations—it'll make your builds look much more interesting! For instance, a cabin made of wood will look more realistic if you use different shades of brown and different types of wood grain.

19 There are other options in the Explorer window you can use to change the properties of a part, such as **Reflectance** and **Transparency.**

20 Both of these controls work on a scale of 0 to 1. Reflectance makes things more reflective, Transparency makes them see-through.

21 They're particularly useful if you want to make a realistic-looking window—try making a piece of glass with the Reflectance set to 0.5 and the Transparency to 0.8. You'll have something that's see-through, but you can still tell it's there—and the sun will reflect off it, too.

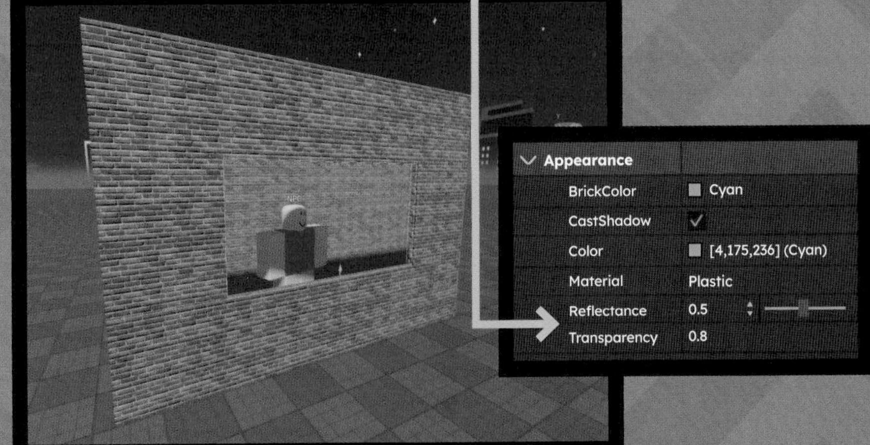

22

Mode: Geometric ▾

Collisions

Join Surfaces

Look on the Model tab, and you'll see two options marked **Collisions** and **Join Surfaces.** Collisions is a particularly useful tool—if it's switched on, then parts won't merge with each other when you move them into the same space. Move a part and when it hits another one, it'll stop.

23 If Collisions is turned off, then you can combine parts to make more intricate shapes—you can create a cylinder with rounded ends by merging spheres into it. Join Surfaces makes two parts join when they meet.

BLOX TIP

Everything in your world is listed in the Explorer window—a new part will have the default name "Part." We recommend giving them more distinctive names—it's much quicker and easier to find things, and helps with scripting, too.

24 Often when building, you'll want more than one of the same part. So you can select a part, hit **Duplicate** up at the top left, and another will appear—in the same place as the original if Collisions isn't on, directly above it if Collisions is on.

25 Once you're happy with a building, you don't want to have to move every part of it individually just to put it a bit closer to the road. This is where the **Group** function comes in. Use Select to highlight your structure, making sure all the parts of it are highlighted, and then click Group.

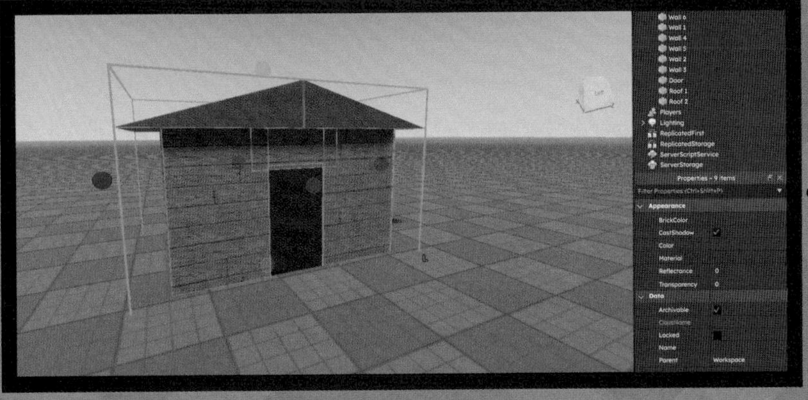

26

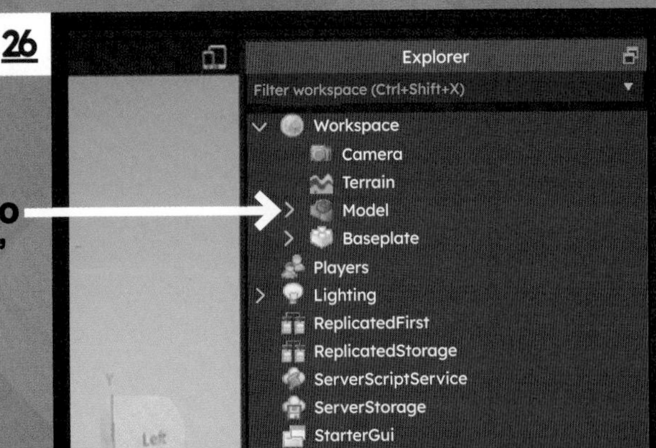

CHANGE TO "HOUSE"

Now all the parts are combined into one. In the Explorer window, this will have the name "Model"; we suggest you rename it to what it actually is, like "House."

27 If you need to move any part of the model, you can use the Group tool to ungroup it, then regroup it when you're done.

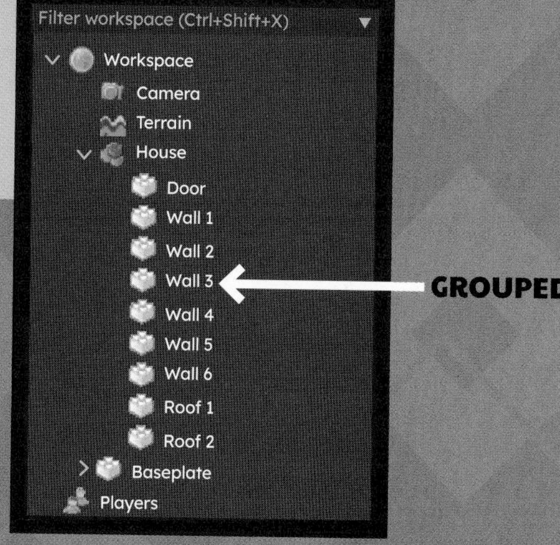

28 You can also duplicate a whole model—so if you want to make a village, you can just make one house and then copy it. Try doing this and then tweaking each house to make them all look a little different!

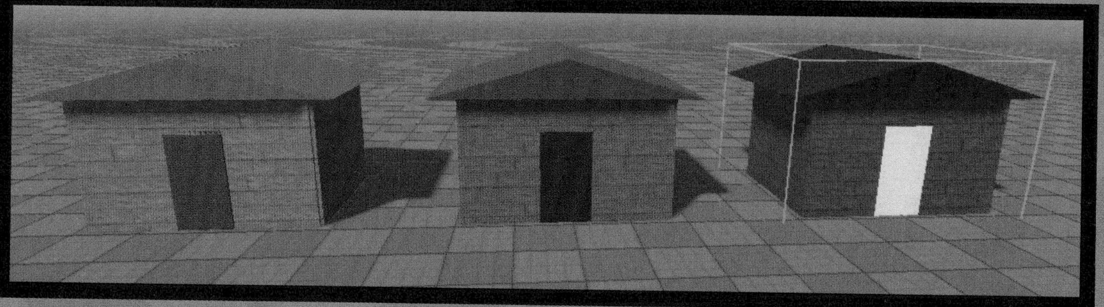

29 One last tip—don't forget you need everything to be the right size for players to interact with. So use Toolbox to put an NPC in your landscape so you keep a good idea of scale, and don't make doors that are too small or tables that are too high!

BLOX TIP

There's a keyboard shortcut you can use to Duplicate even quicker—hold Ctrl and hit D.

FOLLOW THE SCRIPT!

Building your game environment is one thing, but to make it *work* you need scripts.

1 Remember we mentioned the Obby template at the start of this chapter? Open it up and check out those deadly red blocks. These "**killbricks**" have a script attached that kills players who touch them.

2 You can use Roblox Studio to look at any scripts attached to an object. Click on one of the killbricks and go to the Explorer window. Click the arrow next to where it says "Killbrick" and you should be able to see something called "Killscript."

3 Right-click on this and click "Open," and you'll be able to look at the script. This is a very simple script, but it's a good one to start off with.

```
script.Parent.Touched:connect(function(hit)
    if hit and hit.Parent and hit.Parent:FindFirstChild("Humanoid") then
        hit.Parent.Humanoid.Health = 0
    end
end)
```

4 See where it says "hit.Parent.Humanoid.Health = 0"? That's basically saying that the player who touches this thing gets their health reduced to zero.

5 So if you wanted a brick to reduce the player's health to a different amount, you could change that number.
But that's where things get more complicated! You'd need to look at how much health the player had to start with, and you'd probably want it to reduce their health *by* a certain amount, rather than *to* a different amount.

6 But hopefully you're starting to get a sense of how scripts work.

7 One way of using scripts in your games is to copy ones other people have made. Besides being quicker, it can help you learn how they work before you start making your own.

8 For instance, if you want a lava pit in your game, you can copy the killbrick and change its size to make it the surface of the pit. Or, if you've already built your lava pit, you can copy the Killscript and insert that into the part you've used for the surface.

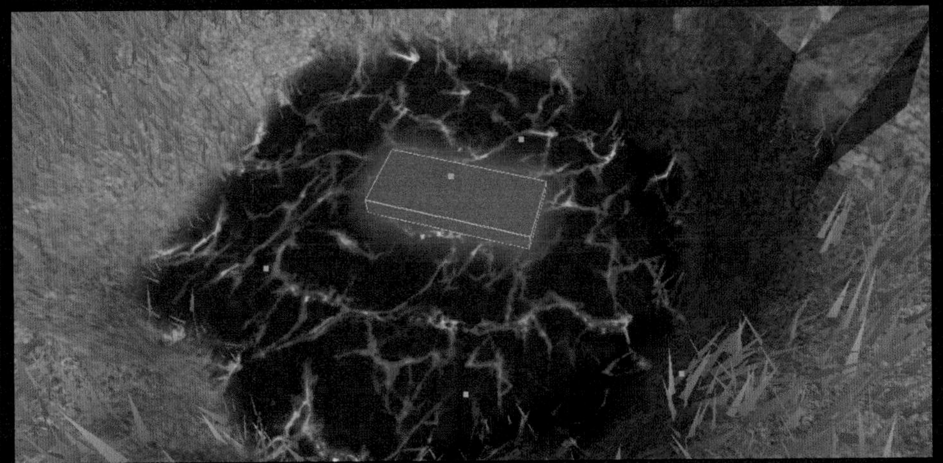

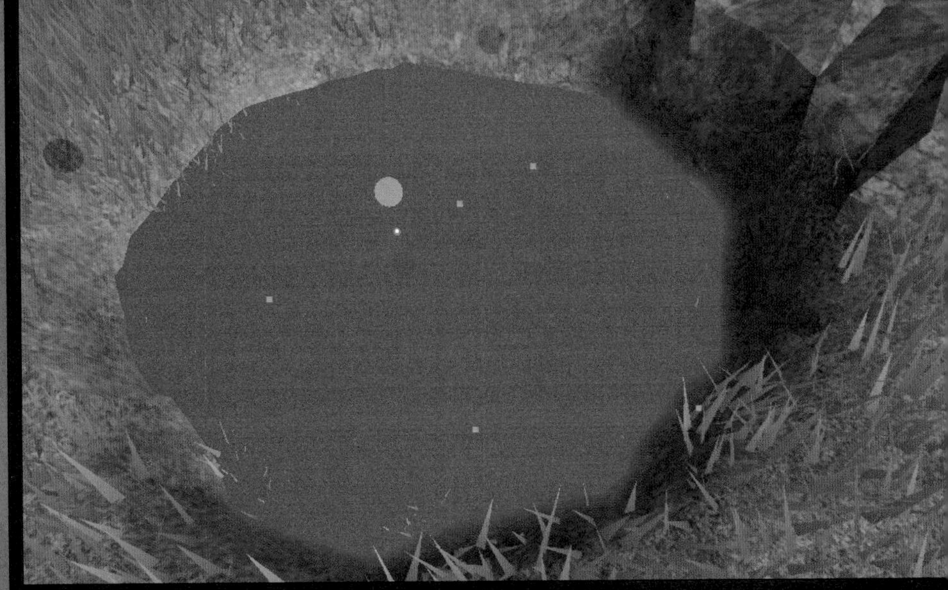

9 If you want to insert a script into a part, just go to the Explorer window, right-click on the script, and copy it. Then go to the part, right-click on it, and click Paste Into.

10 The game templates in Roblox Studio all have scripts that work for that type of game, and you can copy those if they work for the type of game you want to make.

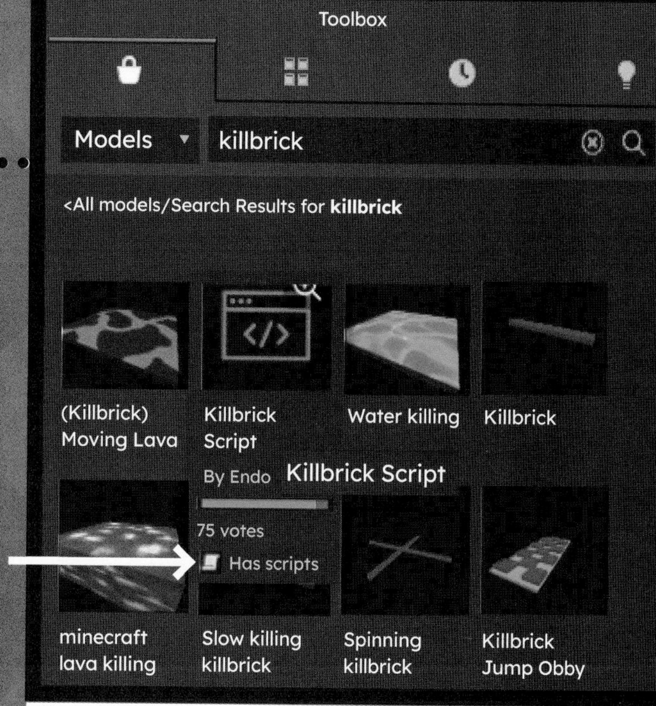

HAS SCRIPTS

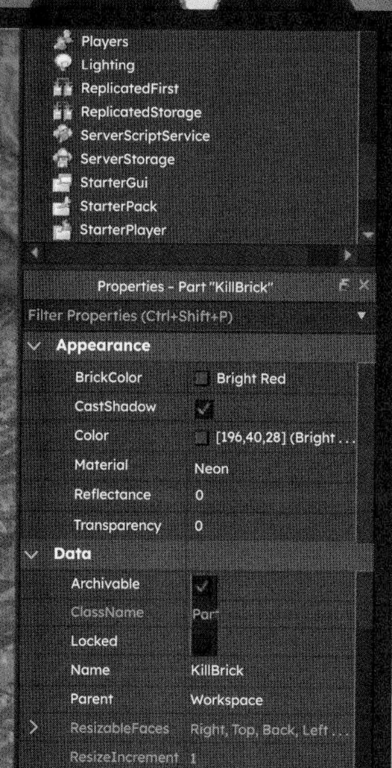

11 There are lots of scripts in the Toolbox, too—so many, in fact, it can be tricky to work out which one works best for what you need. But there's no harm in trying different ones.

BLOX TIP

Many of the objects you'll find in the Toolbox have scripts already built in—you'll see "Has scripts" at the bottom of the description when you hover the mouse over them.

12 Try adding collectibles to your game—like **coins.** A search for "coins" in the Toolbox should bring up a choice of coins with scripts built in. Place one into your game.

13 Now you can look at the scripts built into the coin. You should certainly find a script that deals with what happens when a player touches a coin: The coin should disappear, and an amount should be added to the player's total money.

14 When the coin disappears, what the script will usually do is make its Transparency equal 1 and set its collision to OFF. This means the coin is still "there," but you can't see it or touch it.

```
local db = true
script.Parent.Touched:connect(function(hit)
    if hit.Parent:FindFirstChild("Humanoid") ~= nil then
        if db == true then
            db = false
            script.Parent.Transparency = 1
            local player = game.Players:GetPlayerFromCharacter(hit.Parent)
            player.leaderstats.Coins.Value = player.leaderstats.Coins.Value + 1
            script.Sound:Play()
            script.Parent.Transparency = 1
            wait(1)
            db = true
            script.Parent.Transparency = 0
        end
    end
end)
```

15 A lot of coins come with a **leaderboard script,** which is handy as you'll need something to keep track of how many coins each player has collected.

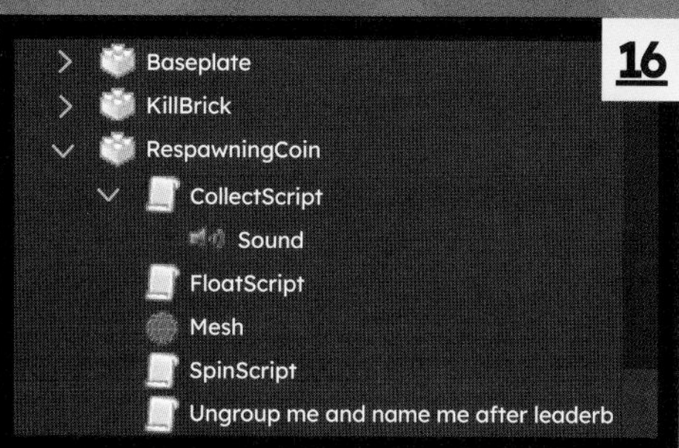

16 And many are also equipped with a **respawning script.** This means the coin will reappear after being collected. The script will contain the information on how long it takes for a coin to respawn—you don't want it to respawn immediately, otherwise players can just collect the same coin over and over again.

17 If you don't want your coins to respawn at all, either choose a coin from the Toolbox that doesn't—or find the respawn part of the script and delete it.

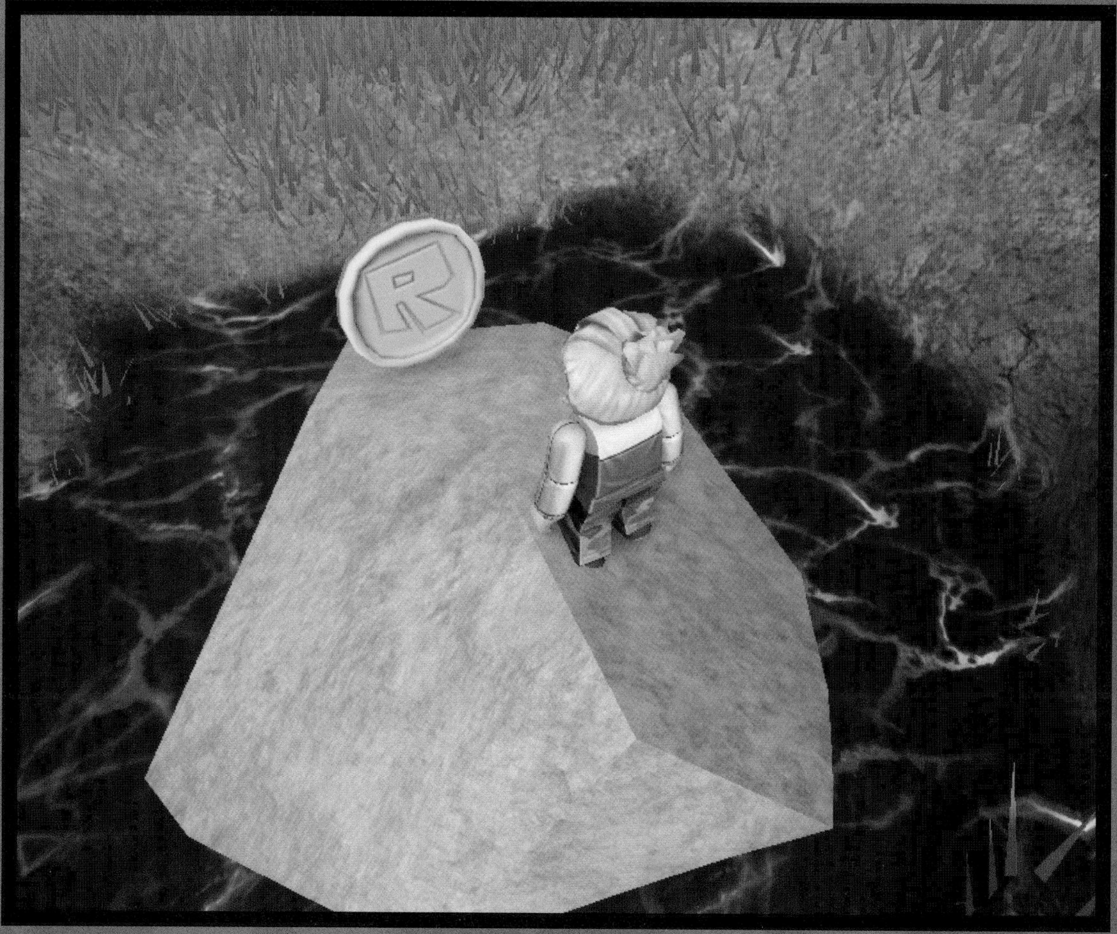

18 Now that you have the coin, you can try changing it to suit your game. When you're making changes to scripts, it's a good idea to test the game regularly and make sure it's doing what you want it to do.

19 Go to the Home tab and use the **Play** option at the end—this should drop your Roblox avatar into the game. If something isn't working, you can undo whatever you just did and try again.

20 First, open the coin's script and see if you can find the part that controls how long the coin takes to respawn. Look for a number in brackets next to the word "wait"—this should be the number of seconds it takes. Change that number to another value.

```
local db = true
script.Parent.Touched:connect(function(hit)
    if hit.Parent:FindFirstChild("Humanoid") ~= nil then
        if db == true then
            db = false
            script.Parent.Transparency = 1
            local player = game.Players:GetPlayerFromCharacter(hit.Parent)
            player.leaderstats.Coins.Value = player.leaderstats.Coins.Value + 1
            script.Sound:Play()
            script.Parent.Transparency = 1
            wait(1)
            db = true
            script.Parent.Transparency = 0
        end
    end
end)
```

21 Now see if you can find the part that controls the value of the coin—it'll probably be on a line of code with the word "value" on it. (It'll help if you've playtested the game and checked how much you get for each coin.) Try changing this and see if it works.

22 The coin may also have scripts to make it float in the air or spin around. Don't mess with these! But if you've managed to make the other changes we suggested, you're ready to try doing something new with these scripts . . .

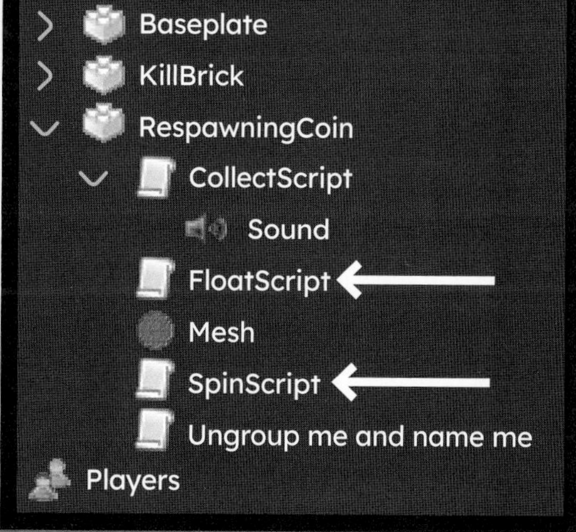

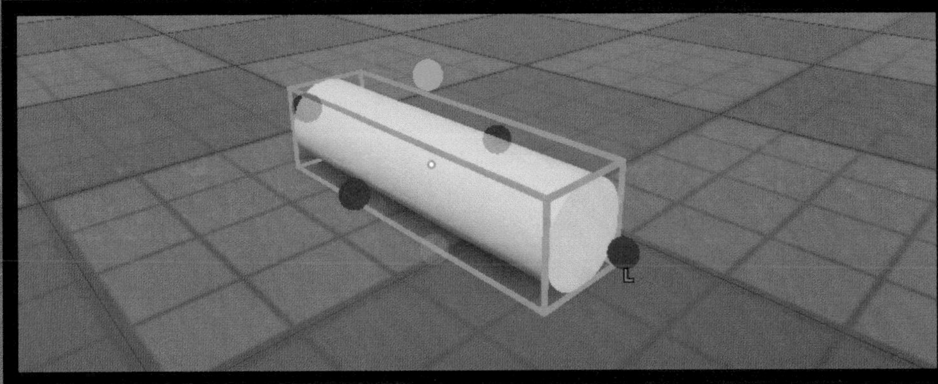

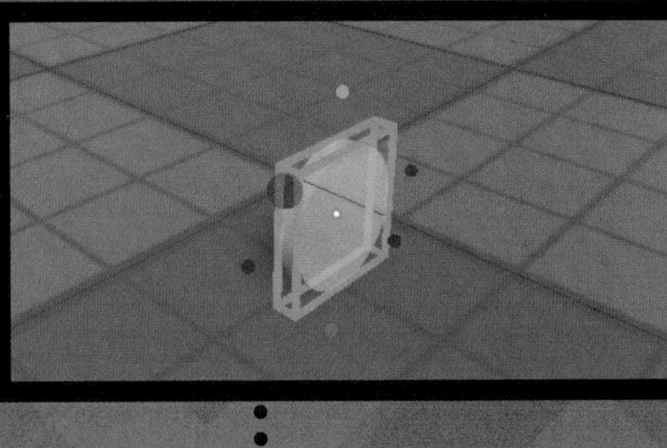

23 First, make a coin of your own by using the "cylinder" part and resizing it to make a disc. (Don't worry if it doesn't look as fancy as the one from the Toolbox, but if you have the skills to make it fancy, go for it!)

24 Make sure Collisions are set to OFF—you want to be able to touch it but also walk through it, if that makes sense. If you want the coin to stay in a particular position, click **Anchor** in the Home tab. Doing that will make the part stay where you put it—otherwise it'll just fall to the ground.

25 Copy the scripts from the coin you got from the Toolbox and paste them into your own coin. (You don't necessarily need to worry about effects like spinning and floating.)

26 Now, here's where it gets interesting! Duplicate your coin and change the color of one of them—maybe one could be silver and the other could be blue.

27 Go into the scripts and give different values to the different coins—maybe 10 for blue and 5 for silver (or the other way around, if you're feeling chaotic).

28 Now put the coins around your game world—the game will be more fun if they're hard to find, so put them in places you can't immediately see them.

29 This makes a very simple game where players compete to collect coins! We suggest you also look through the Toolbox and add a timer—the player with the most money when the time runs out is the winner.

GET TOOLED UP

You need the right tool for the job—so make one!

1 **Tools**—things a player can pick up and use—are a very common feature of games, and they work a bit differently from objects that are just part of the landscape.

2 Again, it'll help you understand how tools work if you get one from the Toolbox and check that out first. So find a **sword** in the Toolbox—the first one that comes up will probably be the one made by Roblox themselves. Check that it has scripts—if it doesn't, it's not really a tool!

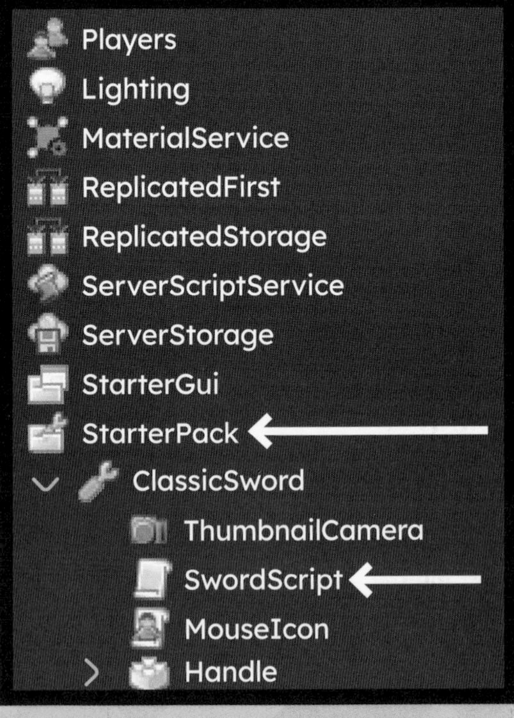

3 Import the sword into your game. Studio should ask you if you want to add it to "StarterPack." This simply means it'll be one of the items a player has when they start a new game.

4 Of course, this isn't the only way you can put tools in the game—players can also acquire them during play. But for now, let's say yes.

5 Go to StarterPack in the Explorer window and look at the sword. It should have a script to control how it works in the game, and also a **handle.** Not all tools need handles, but a weapon like a sword will.

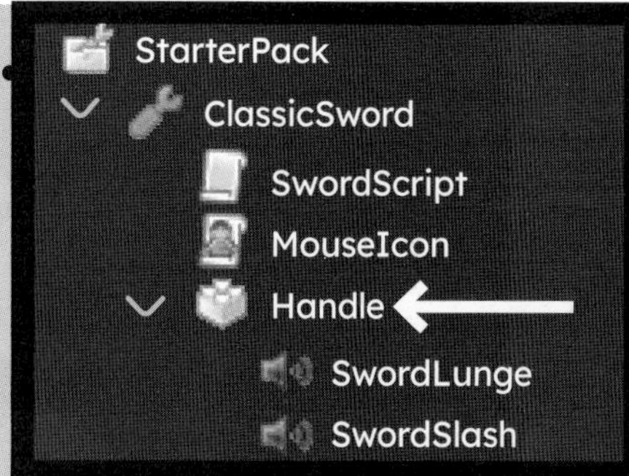

6 It'll probably also have an icon that appears at the bottom of your screen so you can see what tools you've got.

7 Open up the script, and you'll see how complex a simple sword can be! You should find values for the damage it does when it strikes another player, but also animations and any other ways it affects the game.

```
            local Anim = Tool:FindFirstChild("R15Lunge")
            if Anim then
                local Track = Humanoid:LoadAnimation(Anim)
                Track:Play(0)
            end
        end
    end
    --[[
    if CheckIFAlive() then
        local Force = Instance.new("BodyVelocity")
        Force.velocity = Vector3.new(0, 10, 0)
        Force.maxForce = Vector3.new(0, 4000, 0)
        Debris:AddItem(Force, 0.4)
        force.Parent = Torso
    end
    ]]

    wait(0.2)
    Tool.Grip = Grips.Out
    Wait(0.6)
    Tool.Grip = Grips.Up

    Damage = DamageValues.SlashDamage
end

Tool.Enabled = true
LastAttack = 0

function Activated()
    if not Tool.Enabled or not ToolEqipped or not CheckIfAlive() then
        return
    end
    Tool.Enabled = false
    local Tick = RunSerice.Stepped:wait()
    if (Tick - LastAttack < 0.2) then
        Lunge()
    else
        Attack()
    end
    lastAttack = Tick
    --wait(0.5)
```

8 Now let's try making a tool. You don't start by making the model for the tool—you start by making what's called a **container** for the tool.

9 This is because a tool doesn't *necessarily* have to be an object. It might, for instance, be a magic spell or superpower that can be activated. But we're going to make a tool you can hold.

10 Go into the Explorer window and click the plus sign next to Workspace. One of the options that should appear is Tool. Click that, and a new tool container will appear in the Tools folder.

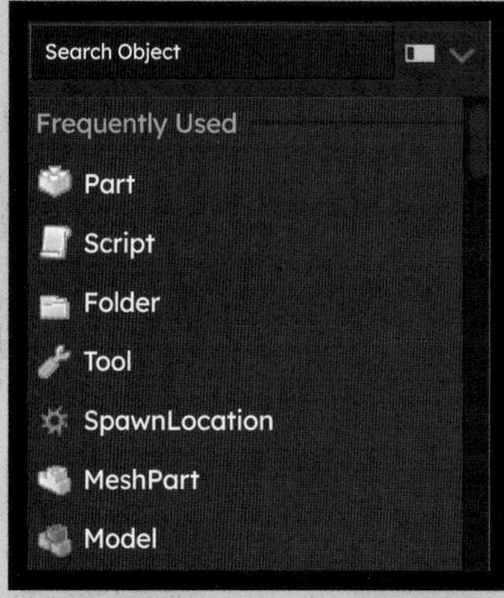

11 Now any part you put into the tool container will become part of the tool. You may find it easiest to use the usual menu to put a part into the workspace, change it to how you want it, and then drag it into the tool container.

TOOL CONTAINER

12 Or you can assemble the whole thing outside of the tool container and drag all the parts in at once.

BLOX TIP

You may have seen the words "parent" and "child" in scripts. A tool is a good example of that—the tool container is the parent, each of the parts inside it is a child.

13 We suggest making something quite simple, like a sword. This can be made out of cylinders. You can try a more elaborate design if you're confident about using Studio.

14 Start by putting one cylinder in place. We're going to make this the handle—go into the Explorer window and change its name from "Part" to "Handle." As you might expect, this is the part the player will hold.

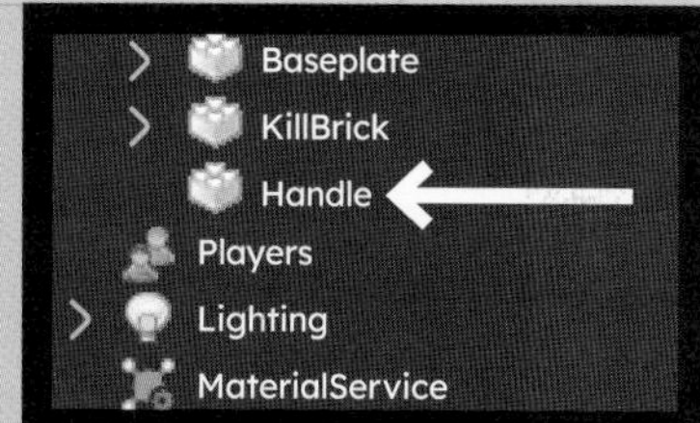

Behavior
CanBeDropped
ManualActivatio. . .
RequiresHandle
State

15 Only do this with one part of your tool—if more than one part is called "Handle," the system will randomly use one of them as the handle. And look in the properties of your tool to make sure the "RequiresHandle" box is ticked.

16 The handle part needs to be **nested** directly under the tool container—this means it can't be under another part or inside another folder that's inside the container. If you're not sure, drag and drop the handle onto the tool container.

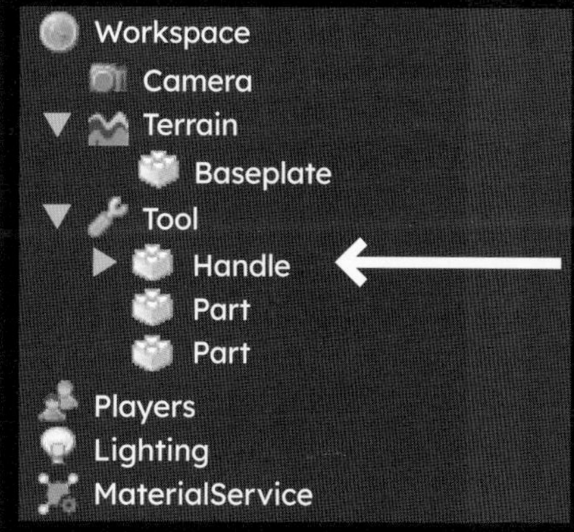

▼ Part	
Anchored	☐
▶ CenterOfMass	0, 0, 0
CustomPhysica . . .	☐
Mass	
Massless	☐
RootPriority	0
Shape	Cylinder

BLOX TIP

Make sure none of the parts of your tool are anchored in place. If they are, the tool won't move—which means the player won't be able to move while holding it!

17 Create another cylinder and join this on to the handle. You need all the parts of your tool to be connected, but don't use the group function to make the parts into a model, as we were doing when making objects.

18 Instead, use Join Surfaces to fix the parts together. This is because you'll want to be able to change the settings for different parts of your tool. If the parts don't weld automatically, click the plus sign next to each part and find the "Weld" setting.

Mode: Geometric
☐ Collisions
☑ Join Surfaces

19 At this point, it's a good idea to test out your tool—make sure the player can pick it up, it's the right size, and the handle works.

20 You may find your tool goes sideways in the player's hand when you want them to hold it upright. If this happens, go out of the test and look at the tool's properties. Go down to **Appearance**, and you should see a list of properties beginning with "Grip."

21 We can't explain exactly how changing these will affect the tool, because they'll affect different tools in different ways. But putting a "1" where there's currently a "0" will make the tool point in a different direction—you may find the X, Y, Z model in the corner of the screen useful here.

▼ Appearance	
▼ GripForward	0, 0, -1
X	0
Y	0
Z	-1
▶ GripPos	0, 0, 0
▶ GripRight	1, 0, 0

22 The backspace/delete key will make the player drop the tool, but if you want to disable this function, untick the "CanBeDropped" box.

23 If you want the player to start with the tool, then drag it down to the StarterPack folder. Or it can be a collectible tool you can place in the game environment for the player to pick up.

24 Now your player can pick up their tool, but they can't do anything with it. We need to add some scripts!

CRACKING THE CODE

Writing your own scripts gives you the power!

1 There are four basic states of a tool—**Equipped, Unequipped, Activated,** and **Deactivated.** The most important of these for this tutorial is Activated—that means when the player has the weapon in their hand and clicks. In other words, it's what the weapon does.

2 Let's make our sword a magic sword, and when the player is holding it they can change night to day and back again. Click the plus next to the tool and insert a script. Then type the following text into the script:

```
local tool = script.Parent
local function onActivate()
end
tool.Activated:Connect(onActivate)
```

3 This is a basic template for the Activated status of a tool, and once you work out some other commands you can use it to program different functions. For now, add some lines so the whole script looks like this:

```
local tool = script.Parent
local function onActivate()
    if game.Lighting.ClockTime >= 8 and game.Lighting.ClockTime <
        16 then

        game.Lighting.ClockTime = 0
    else
        game.Lighting.ClockTime = 12
    end
end
tool.Activated:Connect(onActivate)
```

4 Let's break that down. The third and fourth lines are an instruction to check what time it is in the game. If it's between 8 and 16, that means it's daytime. You'll notice the last word there is "then." That's telling the game what to do next.

```
local tool = script.Parent
local function onActivate()
    if game.Lighting.ClockTime >= 8 and game.Lighting.ClockTime <
        16 then

        game.Lighting.ClockTime = 0
    else
        game.Lighting.ClockTime = 12
    end
end
tool.Activated:Connect(onActivate)
```

5 If it is daytime, the next line of code tells the game it should change the time to 0, meaning midnight.

6 The next line says "else." That's telling the game what to do if it's not between 8 and 16. In that case, it should change the time to 12, meaning midday.

7 Because this is a simple choice between two options—day or night—it's a simple script. Test it out!

KEY SKILLS

Unlock your potential!

1 Let's make something you can use in all kinds of games—especially exploration and survival games. We're going to make a door that can be unlocked with a **key.** You'll have seen doors in Roblox that use animations to open, but for this we're going to keep it simple.

2

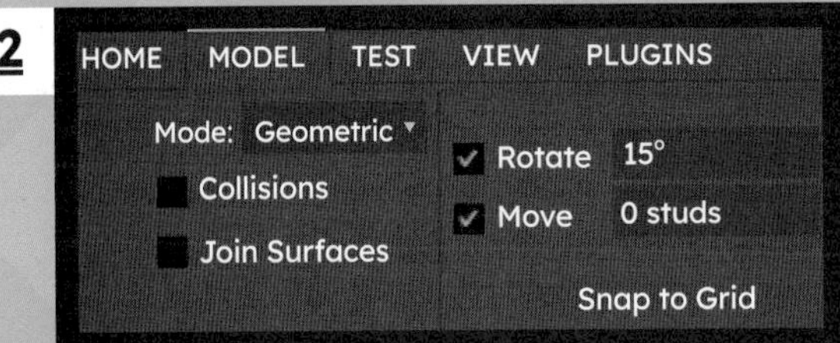

First, open a workspace in Studio and set Collisions and Join Surfaces to OFF.

3 Place a block into your workspace and make it door-shaped. Make it any color and material you like. Go to the Explorer window and rename this block "Door."

4 Look at the properties for this part. Make sure "CanCollide" is ON and the part is anchored.

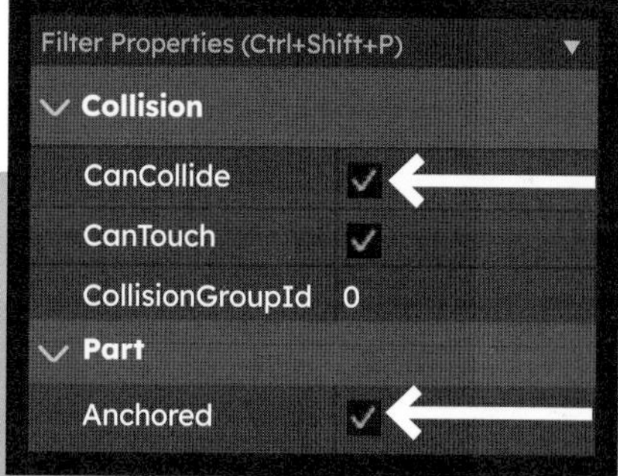

5 Now place a sphere into your workspace, much smaller than the door, and make it a different color. Place it on the door in the right place for a handle. Make sure this part is anchored, but this time, set "CanCollide" to OFF. Rename it "Handle."

6 Duplicate your handle and put it on the other side of the door, then group these three parts and make them into a model. Rename this model "LockedDoor."

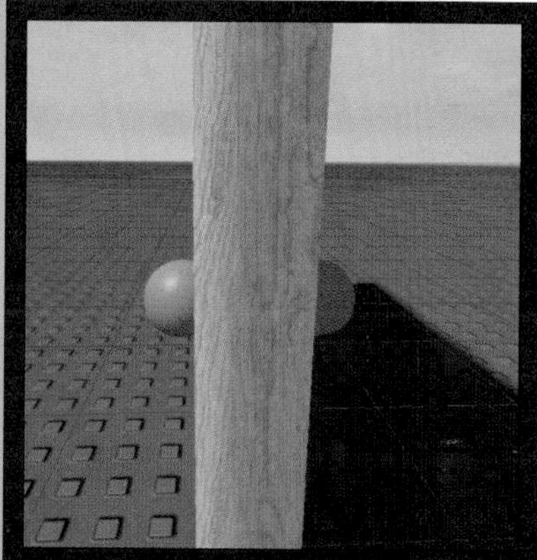

7 Go to the LockedDoor model in the Explorer window and click the plus sign. One of the options should be "StringValue." Use this to add a string value to this part and rename it "Key."

8 Go into the properties of your Key string value and, where it says "Value," type "Key." This is the important part!

Data	
Archivable	✓
ClassName	StringValue
Name	Key
Parent	LockedDoor
Value	Key

Values

- BoolValue
- BrickColorValue
- CFrameValue
- Color3Value
- IntValue
- NumberValue

9 Click the plus sign on the LockedDoor model again, and search for "BoolValue." Add a bool value and rename it "KeyRemove." You don't need to type a value into this one.

10 Now click the plus sign on the Door part and add a script to it. Start by deleting the text that's already there, then type the following:

```
function onTouched(hit)
```

BLOX TIP

That part with the squiggle and the equals sign (~=) means "not equal to."

11 That line tells the script to react when a player touches it. Now we need to tell the script what to do next.

```
if hit.Parent:findFirstChild("Humanoid") ~= nil then
    if game.Players:findFirstChild(hit.Parent.Name) ~= nil

    then

        if

            hit.Parent:findFirstChild(script.Parent.Parent.Key.Value) ~= nil
        then

            if script.Parent.Parent.KeyRemove.Value == true

            then

                hit.Parent:findFirstChild(script.Parent.Parent.Key.Value):remove()

            end
```

12 All of this is checking whether you have a key, so let's tell the script what to do if you do have one. A script's "Parent" is the thing you've placed the script into—in this case, that's the part called "Door." We can use this to make a script change the properties of that thing, like this:

```
script.Parent.Transparency = 0.8
```

13 This is a simple alternative to animating a door opening and closing. The script is telling the door to become almost transparent: It won't completely disappear, but the player will be able to see through to the other side.

BLOX TIP

If you want, you can choose a different value for the door. Entering 1 instead of 0.8 will make it completely transparent—though the handle will just sort of hang there . . .

14 The next part is even more important:

```
script.Parent.CanCollide = false
```

15 By changing "CanCollide" to "false," we make it so the player can walk through the door.

16 Now, we don't want the door hanging around being all semi-transparent, so let's add something to the script that'll make the door come back after a brief interval. Type:

```
wait(2)
```

17 The number 2 is the number of seconds the game will wait before taking the next action. It doesn't have to be 2, but we figure this is a decent amount of time for the player to walk through the door. Next, type:

```
script.Parent.Transparency = 0
script.Parent.CanCollide = true
```

18 These are the values the door had before it was unlocked—transparency is 0, so you can't see through it, and collisions are set to "CanCollide," meaning you can't just walk through it. This sets it back to how it was.

19 The scripting tool will probably add "end" as you add lines to the script, but if they're not there, you should have four. Then type one last line:

```
            end
        end
    end
end
script.Parent.Touched:connect(onTouched)
```

20 So to recap, your Door script should look like this:

```
function onTouched(hit)
    if hit.Parent:findFirstChild("Humanoid") ~= nil then
       if game.Players:findFirstChild(hit.Parent.Name) ~= nil

       then

           if

               hit.Parent:findFirstChild(script.Parent.Parent.Key.Value) ~= nil
           then

               if script.Parent.Parent.KeyRemove.Value == true

               then

                   hit.Parent:findFirstChild(script.Parent.Parent.Key.Value):remove()

               end
               script.Parent.Transparency = 0.8
               script.Parent.CanCollide = false
               wait(2)
               script.Parent.Transparency = 0
               script.Parent.CanCollide = true
           end
       end
   end
end
script.Parent.Touched:connect(onTouched)
```

21 But we're still missing something—the key! You can make your own key if you like—just make sure you set it up as a tool if you do. For this exercise we're going to find a key from the Toolbox—again, it needs to be a tool because then the players will be able to pick it up.

22 Now test it out! You should find the door is impossible to pass if you don't have the key. With the key, you should be able to get through.

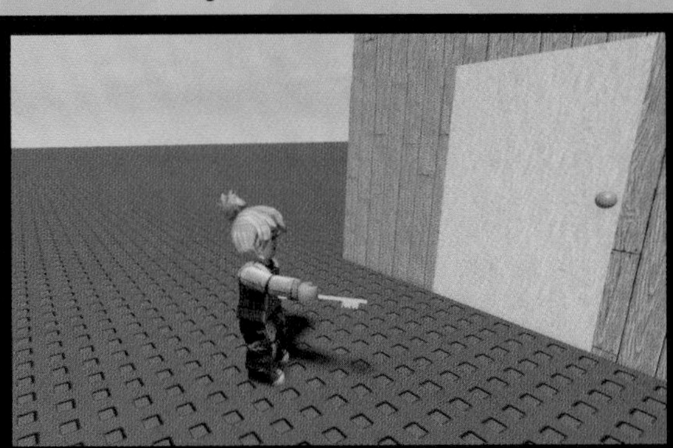

23 Well done on making your unlockable door! But if you want to put this into a game, there's a slight problem: The player still has the key after walking through the door, and can use it to open any doors they encounter after that. That's too easy.

24 What we need are keys that only open particular doors—you know, like real keys do. You can do this by changing a few parts of the code.

25 First duplicate your door and key, and move them away from the original door and key. Then rename the new key "Key2."

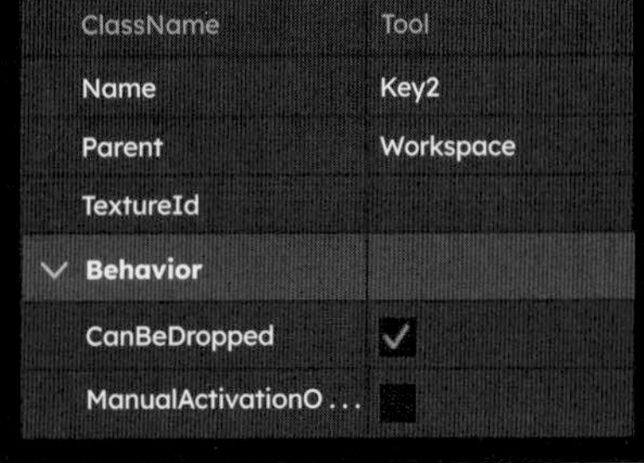

26 Now open the script inside the new door. It should be exactly the same as the script you wrote for the first one. Look for the two parts that say:

```
hit.Parent:findFirstChild(script.Parent.Parent.Key.Value):remove()
```

27 Change them to:

```
hit.Parent:findFirstChild(script.Parent.Parent.Key2.Value):remove()
```

28 Finally, go to this door's string value. Rename it "Key2" and go into its properties. Change the value to "Key2" as well.

```
function onTouched(hit)
    if hit.Parent:findFirstChild("Humanoid") ~= nil then
        if game.Players:findFirstChild(hit.Parent.Name) ~= nil

        then

            if

                hit.Parent:findFirstChild(script.Parent.Parent.Key2.Value) ~= nil
            then

                if script.Parent.Parent.KeyRemove.Value == true

                then

                    hit.Parent:findFirstChild(script.Parent.Parent.Key2.Value):remove()

                end
                script.Parent.Transparency = 0.8
                script.Parent.CanCollide = false
                wait(2)
                script.Parent.Transparency = 0
                script.Parent.CanCollide = true
            end
        end
    end
end
script.Parent.Touched:connect(onTouched)
```

```
Filter workspace (Ctrl+Shift+X)
Workspace
    Camera
    Terrain
    Key
    Key2
    LockedDoor
    LockedDoor
        Key2
        KeyRemove
        Door
            Script
        doorhandle 1
        doorhandle 2
    Union
    Union
    Baseplate
    Part
Players
Lighting
MaterialService
ReplicatedFirst
```

29 Test it out. You should find that picking up the second key will let you open the second door but not the first, while the first key will unlock the first door but not the second. (The player will need to equip the right key for each door—you might want to make the keys droppable by ticking the "CanBeDropped" box.)

30 Make some cool environments and put a good story behind it, and this could be a really fun Roblox game!

FREQUENTLY ASKED QUESTIONS

How can I get free Robux?

You can't! Loads of people online promise free Robux—these are all scams. You can, however, earn Robux.

Okay, how can I earn Robux?

By creating things in Roblox and offering them for sale. If you've created a game, you can charge Robux for access—but there are so many free experiences on Roblox, most people will just go and do something free instead. It's more common to make a free game that features in-game purchases. But focus on making an entertaining game first!

What if I don't want to make a whole game?

You can make clothes and offer those for sale, as we explained earlier on—but you'll have to pay a small Robux fee to upload them.

What if I want to add music to my game?

It's possible to upload music files to Roblox Studio, but only do this if either you made it yourself or you have permission to use it from the person who did. If you don't have permission, your game could fall victim to a copyright strike. There's lots of copyright-free music made by Roblox—search the toolbox for audio and set the creator to ROBLOX.

What are plugins, and how do I use them?

Plugins add extra functions to Roblox Studio that aren't part of the usual setup. You can find them in the Toolbox: For example, you can get one that adds rain to your game or that makes the corners of your blocks rounded. Once you've installed a plugin, you can choose whether it's active or not.

How do I let other people play my game?

It's very easy—just go to the My Experiences tab on the website and click the icon under the name of the game you want to make available. If you change this to "public," everyone will be able to see and play your game.

HOTTEST GAMES QUIZ ANSWERS

1	A ninja.
2	A roof.
3	400 Robux.
4	5,000.
5	Level 20.
6	*Dragon Ball, My Hero Academia*, or *Attack on Titan* are all good answers!
7	A gacha system.
8	On a grind rail.
9	By paying 100 Robux.
10	Quill Lake.

WEIRD GAMES QUIZ ANSWERS

1. *Minecraft.*
2. The Nicki Minaj badge.
3. Meerkat Mode.
4. Bacons.
5. Three.
6. Mermaid Potion.
7. Three.
8. Pizza.
9. EMOTIONAL DAMAGE!!
10. Timothy.

HORROR GAMES QUIZ ANSWERS

1. Survive all the floors.
2. Up to eight.
3. SpongeBob Squarepants.
4. Teke Teke.
5. The hunter.
6. Discs to play in the laptop.
7. 2009.
8. Eight.
9. Shop, spectate, goof around with cannons.
10. January 2020.

HIDDEN GEMS QUIZ ANSWERS

1. It's frozen over.
2. Any two from fire, water, air, or electricity.
3. Punching.
4. The Grimwood.
5. Cards.
6. Viruses and Malware.
7. Four.
8. Pulling up your hood.
9. The Angel's Chosen.
10. The International Space Station.

MY FAVORITE ROBLOX GAMES

MY FAVORITE GAME IS ....

MY FAVORITE GENRE IS ....

MY FAVORITE DEVELOPER IS ....

MY FAVORITE HOT GAME IS ....

MY FAVORITE WEIRD GAME IS ....

MY FAVORITE HORROR GAME IS ....

MY FAVORITE HIDDEN GEM IS ....

MY FAVORITE ROBLOX STUDIO GAME TEMPLATE IS ....